DECENTRALISED GOVERNANCE AND PARTICIPATORY DEVELOPMENT

About the Author

Mohanan Bhaskaran Pillai (*b.* 1957) is a senior faculty in Political Science and Development Administration, Gandhigram Rural Institute, Gandhigram, Tamil Nadu. He has founded the Institute for the Study of Developing Areas in Trivandrum, Kerala in 1991 along with a host of other independent thinkers. He is the founder Editor (Hon.) of *ISDA Journal*—Studies in Development and Administration. He specialises in development administration, South Asian Studies and Political Theory. He has published several books, research papers and articles on South Asian Development issues. His major books include *Politics of Regionalism in South Asia* (1991); *Globalisation of Economy* (1995); *Gandhi's Legacy and a New Human Civilisation* (1999); *Quest for a Just World Order* (1999) and *Women and Law* (2003).

He has participated and presented papers at international conferences organised by Association of Third World Studies Inc. and International Institute of Asian Studies, The Netherlands. In addition, he has organised several national conferences, workshops and seminars in Gandhigram and Trivandrum.

DECENTRALISED GOVERNANCE AND PARTICIPATORY DEVELOPMENT

Issues, Constraints and Prospects

B. MOHANAN

CONCEPT PUBLISHING COMPANY, NEW DELHI-110059

ISBN-81-8069-162-4

First Published 2005

Published and printed by

Ashok Kumar Mittal
Concept Publishing Company
A/15-16, Commercial Block, Mohan Garden,
NEW DELHI-110059 (India)

Phones : 25351460, 25351794
Fax : 0091-11-25357103
E-mail : publishing@conceptpub.com

PREFACE

The Communist Party of India (Marxist) controlled Left Democratic Front (LDF). Government of Kerala took the decision of political and financial devolution of powers to Local Self-Governments in an unprecedented way and thus added a new dimension to the 73rd and 74th Amendments (1993) to the Constitution of India which was considered by advocates of democratic decentralisation as the most revolutionary piece of legislation in the constitutional history of India since independence. Simultaneously, the government decided to ensure the participation of the people at the bottom line in the formulation and implementation of the 9th Plan in Kerala and to make people's participation in development planning a permanent feature of the planning process in Kerala. These bold steps of Kerala's left government attracted the attention of academics and planners from all over the world and therefore, Development Researchers and Activists have been visiting Local Self-Government Institutions (LSGIs) in Kerala to have a closer understanding of the process of peoples' plan. At the same time the programme was not free from criticism. The then opposition Congress(I) and its allies considered the campaign as an attempt from the part of the CPI(M) to pump public money into the hands of local cadres of that party. In the totally polarized bi-party pattern of coalition politics such criticism is quite natural.

The CPI(M) in this context stated that they are interested in a consensus to address the developmental issues of the state and looking towards the Congress(I) to bring in a new development culture in Kerala.

However, the kind of development culture as conceptualised by E.M.S. Namboodiripad, the architect of People's Plan Movement is not easy as is evident from the attitude of the Congress(I) as opposition party in the past four years in Kerala and as the ruling party for the last two years. The attitude of Congress(I) led United Democratic Front (UDF) Government towards Democratic Decentralisation and planning from below is lukewarm. Immediately after coming to power the UDF government stated that Panchayats would not get more than 17.5 per cent of the total outlay of the 10th Plan. This is in place of 40 per cent allocation by the previous LDF Government. The UDF Government led by Congress leader A.K. Antony has taken some other retrograde steps also. The DRDA which was amalgamated with the District Panchayats by the LDF Government was re-established as separate entity by the UDF government. Similarly Rural Development Department and Panchayat Department which the LDF Government placed under the same Minister got bifurcated again and placed under two different Ministers in the UDF Government. As a result of this rural development funds would go to BDOs as was the case earlier and thus elected panchayats will not have any role in implementing projects that originate from Rural Development Department. Similarly Tribal Sub-Plan (TSP) which was given to panchayats by the LDF was now taken away by SC/ST Development Minister. He has divested the Panchayat of Special Component Plan (SCP) funds.

Apart from this the Government has decided to constitute separate development authorities for Coast Land Development, Hill Area Development and Urban Development. All these are retrograde steps when viewed from the perspective of decentralised governance and participatory development.

B. MOHANAN

ACKNOWLEDGEMENTS

I am grateful to the authorities of Gandhigram Rural Institute for providing me with funds from the unassigned grant of UGC to undertake this study.

I have undertaken several field visits to both Kudappanakunnu and Karakulam Panchayats. Presidents and Members of these Panchayats extended to me all kinds of cooperation. I have interacted with many people in these two panchayats. They have cooperated with me and readily answered my questions. I express my sincere thanks to one and all in these two Panchayats for making my interaction with them a pleasant experience.

Dr. B.S. Bhargava, former Prof. and Head, Development Administration Unit, Institute of Economic and Social Change, Bangalore has gone through the first draft of the study and offered critical comments and valuable suggestions. I have taken his comments seriously and revised certain portions of the study accordingly. I express my sincere thanks to this renowned scholar of Panchayati Raj Studies.

I should also express my gratefulness to Dr. A.S.K. Nair, a Scientist of Centre for Earth and Science Studies, Thiruvananthapuram and Dr.V. Rajendran Nair, Reader in Political Science in VTM NSS College, Thiruvananthapuram for helping at various stages of the study.

Said all these usual disclaimers remain.

Gandhigram

B. MOHANAN

CONTENTS

1

INTRODUCTION

'People's participation' is the most frequently used term in the literature on development and in the vocabulary of its practitioners including donor agencies and NGOs, roughly for the past twenty years. People's participation in development got such greater attention by everyone concerned because of the near total failure of conventional developmental approaches to deliver goods to the target groups. International Development Agencies and UN and its affiliated agencies supported actively development initiatives which ensured people's participation. International donors and development organizations found NGOs as the locomotives of development with popular participation.

In India people's participation in development emerged as a favourite theme in the context of the widely noted failure of community development projects and a critique of the five year plans for its over departmentalism which prevented the benefits of planned development to the poorer sections of the Indian society. It was against this background that the new local self-government system was introduced by amending the Constitution of India. The Local Self-Government Institutions (LSGIs) that came into existence as a result of the 73rd and 74th Amendments to the Constitution and the conformity State Acts provided ample opportunities for a departure from the conventional practice of development.

Taking cue from this, the leftists-controlled state government in Kerala launched a massive programme for ensuring people's participation in the 9th Plan of the state. This unprecedented initiative of Kerala Government caught international attention. Back home it received both laurels and brickbats.

According to the State Planning Board, this bold initiative of political and economic decentralisation combined with grassroots level people's participation was taken to address the developmental crisis that Kerala has been confronting for the past two decades. Through this programme the CPI(M) wanted to be the harbinger of a new development culture in the state beyond partisan politics.

Opponents, mainly the Congress(I) party found in this initiative an attempt from the part of CPI(M) to strengthen the grassroots level cadres of CPI(M). The widely circulated accusation was that in the name of people's participation in development, public money was channelled to the local level cadres of CPI(M). In between the arguments and counter-arguments, accusations and counter-accusations, people's plan campaign completed four years under the state government of the Left coalition and the fifth year under a state government controlled by the Congress(I) led United Democratic Front (UDF). The major objective of the present study is to understand the gap, if any, between the existing theory and Kerala's practice of people's participation. In other words, in what way the Kerala experiment would help us enrich or reconstruct the existing theory of people's participation. Another major objective of the present study is to assess the extent to which this programme succeeded in fulfilling its declared objectives.

Participation: The Concept

Development community has been discussing about various aspects of people's participation in development for the past two decades. Development theorists and practitioners have designed certain strategies also for ensuring people's participation in development projects. The near total failure of 'top-down' approach to development projects in Third World Countries compelled development thinkers to search for alternative strategies for development. Thus emerged the concept of People's Participation. However, the concept is not all new. The Greek philosopher Aristotle discussed the existence of a clear relationship between the extent of participation and the creation of good life. According to Aristotle the best state is one where there existed broad participation and with no class dominating the others. Aristotle also mentioned the relationship between participation and development. However in the development literature it got a place in the fag end of the 1960s. The concept which appeared in the scene at the end of 1960s as an alternative paradigm of development intervention, slowly emerged in the 1970s, acquired strength in the 1980s and made its powerful presence felt in the 1990s, both in theory and practice. In the 1990s people's participation has got strengthened into a well established principle of development which has received support from governments, international development agencies, non-governmental organisations and has been implemented across the sectors in many different countries (Oakley 1995). On the eve of the dawn of the new millennium, people's participation has emerged as the dominant paradigm in development intervention across sectors and countries. This has created a new situation. Currently the talk everywhere is about the participation of people in everything. Participation in research, planning, implementing, monitoring, training and what not! Participation is such an all embracing concept which appears to have been taken up in one form or another by almost every kind of actor in the development process, that the potential for debate and disagreement is endless (*ibid.*).

In fact, the widespread application and debate produced many strands of interpretation and practice of participation over the past three decades. It would be very interesting to have a look at these different strands of interpretations. Pardha Saradhi (1989) discusses the aspects of participation in its four dimensions, *viz*., participation in decision-making, participation in implementation, participation in benefits and participation in evaluation. Of these four dimensions of participation, the first three were identified in a Conference held at MIT in 1968. The fourth one was later added by the Cornell University Rural Development Committee. These four kinds of participation are quite distinct from one another both in respect of activities and structure of participation.

Participation in decision-making is viewed as a process rather than a single act at a particular point in time. It has also been recognized that it has different stages such as generation of ideas, formulation and assessment of options making choice about them as well as the formulation of plans for putting selected options into effect. In this context we have to keep in mind the three different types of decisions, *viz.* initial decisions, on going decisions and operational decisions. Participation of the people can be sought in all these different types of decisions.

Similarly, participation in the implementation process involves : (a) resource contribution, (b) administration and coordination efforts, and (c) programme enlistment activities.

Participation in benefits includes distribution of benefits from development projects on the basis of equality. A development project can lead to a minimum of three kinds of benefits, *viz.*, material, social and personal. People's participation in evaluation can also be of three types, *viz.*, project centred evaluation, political activities and public opinion efforts.

A participatory approach to development should evolve strategies for effective participation of people in all the four dimensions discussed above. Cohen and Uphoff considered participation as "generally denoting the involvement of a significant number of persons in situations or actions which enhance their well-being, *e.g.* their income, security or self-esteem" (as cited in Santhanam 1993). In the context of development "community participation refers to an active process whereby beneficiaries influence the direction and execution of development projects rather than merely receive a share of project benefits"—writes Paul (*ibid.*). The view expressed by ILO is that "participation involved active, collectively organised and continued efforts by the people themselves in setting goals, pooling resources together and taking actions which aim at improving their living conditions". The ACC Task force on rural development defined the term in this way: "What gives real meaning to popular participation is the collective effort by the people concerned to pool their efforts and whatever other resources they decide to pool together to attain the objectives they set for themselves". [ACC Task Force on Rural Development, Report of the Third Meeting of the Working Group on Programme Harmonisation, Rome 1978 as quoted by M.L. Santhanam, "Community Participation for Sustainable Development". *Indian Journal of Public Administration,* Vol. XXXIX, No. 3, 1993, p. 419.] The task force has discussed participation in its active and passive dimensions. What is quoted above represents the active process of participation. Passive process of participation means the involvement of people in development programmes designed and controlled by others.

M.L Santhanam defines participation as "commitment on the part of the individual towards all forms of actions by which the individual can "take part" or "play a role" in the operation without being conscious of any socio-economic barriers to achieve certain common goals in a group situation", (Santhanam 1993:419). This means that to make participation effective, "People of all class and caste should be involved in all stages of plan process". Further, "to effectively participate, persons/group have to identify themselves with the movement. This would be possible only when people are involved in need identification, fixing priorities among the needs and associated in the planning, decision-making, implementing and evaluation process and given an opportunity to create/maintain/manage local organisations" (*ibid.*).

Santhanam made an attempt to identify the factors that influence participation of people in any development programme. These factors are mainly behavioural in nature. The first factor is "the feeling of being consulted" at the time of formulating the proposal and subsequently in the course of action on it. Second factor is "mutual respect" or feeling of a certain prestige. Thirdly, a psychological sense of satisfaction of being a member in a group and fourthly, economic benefit that could be derived out of the project. The author further says that people would decide to participate based on their assessment about the extent to which it would contribute to their goals and the larger interest of the community (*ibid.* :420-21). In other words, an individual would make a comparison of the cost to be incurred and the gain to be accrued. Based on this assumption, Bryant and White proposed the formula given below:

$$Pz = (B \times Pr) - C$$

where Pz = Participation which depends on,

B = Benefits which one hopes to get,

Pr = Probability that they will actually achieve the benefit, and

C = Costs involved to work for the projects.

(Bryant and White 1984 as cited in Santhanam)

This formula predicted that people would participate in a development project if they sensed the possibility of benefits outweighed time and effort (*ibid.*). Santhanam cautions that this formula should not be construed as a trick of making people participate. However, this provides valuable insights into formulating certain basic principles of participation. They are:

1. People organise best around the problems they consider most important in assessing needs and in planning initiatives to meet those needs.

2. Local people make rational economic decision in the context of their own environment and circumstances.

3. Voluntary commitment of labour time, material and money to a project is both an evidence of participation and a necessary condition for breaking patterns of development paternalism.

4. Local control over the amount, quality and distribution of benefits increases the chances of the project becoming self-sustainable.

These clues helped Santhanam to identify following approaches that could be adopted for enlisting community participation.

1. People should be made aware of the details of all the schemes.

2. Identification of felt needs of the people/community need to be done along with the involvement of the people.

3. The planning process should be of "bottom up" approach. The user of the programme should also be the decision maker in the programme.

4. Developing a sense of ownership and responsibility for a programme among the community members creates a feeling of possessiveness. To develop this, the outside agency should be prepared to gradually withdraw its role, delegating responsibility and functions to the community.

5. Subsidy should be given only to serve as supplement to the existing resources of individual/community. A subsidy is most effective, if the individual/community takes it as a form of recognition

of the efforts and that it is aimed at stimulating more effective and sustaining development.

Purpose of Participation

S.N. Mishra (1993) equates people's participation with community participation and defines it as participation in planning, implementation and monitoring of such activities. Mishra then lists out the purposes of participation in the following way:

1. The most important purpose of participation is to create will and determination among the members of the community to improve upon their present and future life.

2. To identify and develop the local resources to generate self-reliance among members of the community.

3. To achieve integrated area development by coordinating among various agencies interested in sustainable development activities.

4. To mobilize available human resources for productive and meaningful activities.

5. Being in constant touch to make the members aware of the community above the development in the area.

6. To help the community to understand the new technology by way of arranging functional literacy programmes.

7. To create centres for discussion and development by organizing various clubs of youth and women.

8. To provide an open forum to the members of the community where they could discuss their problems and find indigenous solutions which may prove efficient and economical.

9. For continuous education and mobilisation of the people in the area to develop local leadership.

10. For accelerating socio-economic development of the community to encourage people to adopt modern changes.

11. To arrange extra-curricular activities for generating social awareness by way of well-designed publicity.

12. To encourage people to develop their own confidence instead of depending upon the government and become self-reliant which is key to development.

Process of Participation

On the basis of the purposes of participation as listed above, Mishra explains the process of participation. He equates the process of participation with participative management. Then he identifies the prerequisites of participative management. The first prerequisite is the understanding of the community itself. Secondly, identification of the priority needs of the community. In the need identification work, opinion leaders of the community should be involved. Thirdly, designing of development programmes and educating the people through formal and informal channels about the usefulness and potentialities of the programme. At this stage an assessment of the locally available resources, involving no cost or very little cost, is to be done by the development workers. The fourth prerequisite is the leadership role of the development workers. The development workers should be properly trained in the art and science of participatory management. The success and failure of a participatory management programme by and large depend upon the leadership role, and administrative capability of the development workers. They should also be persons of vision, initiative and desire. Mishra has summarized his ideas on participatory management in two charts.

Oakley (1995) brought into one single text the many conceptual and practical dimensions of participation by drawing materials from the researches the author has undertaken for institutions such as WHO, FAO and ILO.

The author writes that people's participation has become a dominant theme in the literature on development and within the framework for development programmes in the context of the democratisation process in different parts of the world starting with the tumultuous political changes in eastern Europe. Ever since the powerful convergence of the notion of participation two broadly different schools of thought have been noted by the development community:

Chart : 1

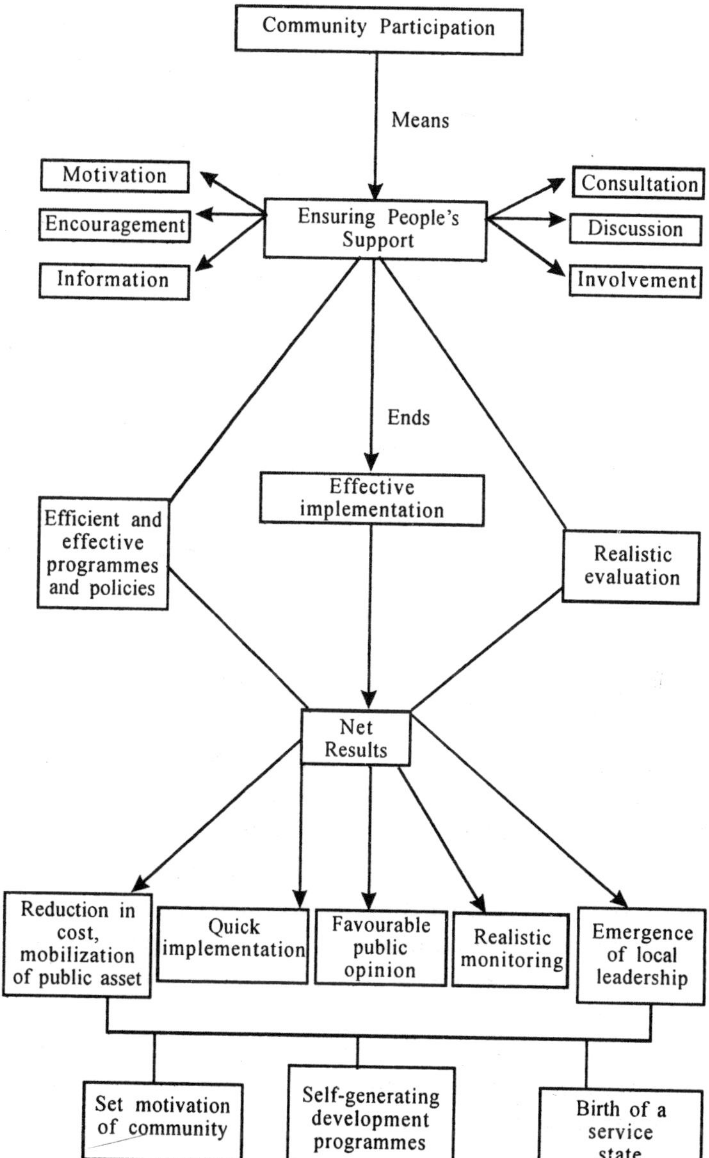

Source : S.N. Mishra, "Peoples Participation for Sustainable Development", *Indian Journal of Public Administration*, Vol. : XXXIX, No. 3, 1993, p. 430.

Chart:2

Analysis of the needs and requirements of the community.
Understanding the positive as well as negative attitudes of the members of the community with regard to various practices with the involvement of the people, designing the development programmes as per their needs and requirements.
Through formal and informal channels educating the people and make them aware of the programmes and utilizing the resources available with them.
With aided guidance leaving the programme to the care of the people.
Handling over the programme to the people and removing the aided guidance.
To sort out problems, if any, occasional follow up is needed.
Birth of community managed sustainable development programmes.
Birth of a service state.

Source : S.N. Mishra, p.433.

1. One school saw "participation" as the key to the inclusion of human resource in development efforts; previously development planners had overlooked the contributions that people could make and the skills that they could bring to development projects. If, therefore, one could incorporate the human element in such projects and persuade people to participate in them, then there would be a stronger chance that these projects would be successful.

2. The other school saw this "participation" in a very different light—as more linked to tackling the structural causes of people's poverty, rather than as yet another input into a development project. People are poor because they are excluded and have little influence upon the forces which affect their livelihoods. Participation is part of the process whereby such people seek to have some influence and to gain access to the resources which would help them sustain and improve their living standards.

Interpretations of People's Participation

Researches carried out by eminent scholars, like Freire (1972),

Elliot (1976), Rolling (1978), Crouch and Chamala (1979) and Peasse brought to light the way that majority in different parts of the world had been excluded from the fruits of social development and economic growth. Later Haque *et al.* (1977), Devitt (1980), Chambers (1981), Kortan and Alfonsa (1981) and the studies of FAO (1986) and World Bank (1992) conceptualized participation in terms of strategies to rectify the imbalances in development by focusing on the problem of poverty. These studies and the practice of people's participation produced mainly the following interpretations of people's participation (Oakley, 1995).

Participation as a Basic Human Right

The interpretation that has influenced many development agencies is the one agreed at the World Conference on Agrarian Reforms and Rural Development (WCARRD) in 1979.

"Participation by the people in the institutions and systems which govern their lives is a basic human right and also essential for realignment of political power in favour of disadvantaged groups and for social and economic development. Rural development strategies can realise their full potential only through the motivation, active involvement and organisation at the grassroots level of rural people, with special emphasis on the least advantaged, in conceptualising and designing policies and programmes and increasing administrative, social and economic institutions, including cooperative and other voluntary forms of organisation for implementing and evaluating them".

Participation as Collaboration

In less developed countries people would come forward voluntarily or as a result of some persuasion to collaborate with an externally determined project. Here people's participation is a programme sponsored by the government or some development organisation. In this kind of participation programmed as part of project input people may be participating in the development project in the sense of collaboration but they could rarely get a chance in designing the project and managing it.

Participation as Organisation

There is no disagreement among the development community that organisation basis is the fundamental requirement for effective participation. At the same time there is disagreement about the nature and evolution of organisation. In most cases organisation is conceived and implanted in the rural areas from outside to ensure people's participation in development activities. In certain cases organisation emerge automatically as an outcome of the process of participation. It is widely recognized that indigenously emerging organisations are successful and become authentic vehicles of people's participation.

Participation as Empowerment

Participation is also interpreted as an exercise of empowering people. As we have already noted in 1979 WCARRD recognised the transfer of power as implied in the concept of people's participation. Similarly in 1980 one major study of UNRISD accepted empowerment as its working definition of participation. According to this view participation is "the empowering of excluded groups in order to increase their access to and control over the resources of development".

After summarizing the different interpretations on people's participation, Oakley comes to the conclusion that one single universal definition of the concept is not possible. Then he defines people's participation as an "active process of direct involvement in the political structures which govern national life in the decision-making and implementation procedures of development programmes and projects and most importantly, in the taking of action by people to confront and tackle the issues which affect their livelihoods in a whole range of activities and in many different contexts". To bring more clarity to his definition he views 'people' as "the broad mass of excluded, disadvantaged people, commonly referred to as the rural poor, who exert little influence on the existing political structure, have only limited access to resources for development and who gain little advantage from development interventions".

P.K. Bajpai (1998) is highly critical of the people' participation models experimented in India such as community development programmes, Panchayat Raj, cooperatives, voluntary organisations, Jawahar Rozgar Yojana etc. Bajpai writes: "Though people's participation is a pre-condition for success of development programmes and there must be an in-built mechanism to involve people in their conceptualisation, planning, implementation, monitoring and management of resources (funds). This may increase the efficacy and acceptance of the programme on the one hand and reduce the operational and administrative costs on the other. Yet government and voluntary organisations have not been successful in evolving a precise method of involving the people and therefore many programmes launched with laudable objectives and great expectations start loosing their momentum sooner or later" (Bajpai, 1998:816). He further writes that people's participation in development process has been elusive due to two factors, *viz*. (1) Lack of honesty on the part of NGOs and government, and (2) People's apathy owing to many reasons who more often than not, are either deviated or resisted to join the moves seeking their participation. After identifying the constraints in people's participation, he gives a seven point package to mobilize people to ensure their participation in development.

1. The first thing to do would be to assess the existing community attitudes and practices. Also, steps should be taken to understand the group dynamics and heterogeneous character of the society. There seems to be a deep-rooted tendency to initiate programmes without a full understanding of how the community views the need or the problem. It must be realised that no two communities are same, and serious differences exist between one community and the other in every area of life and behaviour.

2. While assessing the attitudes and practices steps must be taken to identify the supporting and resisting formal and informal groups, organisations, social institutions, opinion leaders and decision making leaders existing in the community. Special attention must be paid to identify the resources of the people and to educate them to understand their needs and problems.

3. The first two steps would enable to develop realistic community oriented plan with thorough consultation with the people. Their suggestions and reservations must be appropriately accommodated in the plan of action. Better would be if individual and household development plans are developed and people motivated to take active part in the process of their own development.

4. Steps must be taken to mobilize resources both internal and external to carry out the programme. People must realise at this stage that ultimate responsibility of supporting the programmes lies with them only and they have to work consistently and collectively towards mobilisation of more and more resources. However, resources need not necessarily be material/financial.

5. The next step would be to set up proper machinery for action and distribute duties among the people. If need be, they may be given necessary training in a formal or informal manner. Division of duties must be done according to the expertise of the people.

6. Having done the above, the group may be ready for action. This stage implies proper motivation and thorough scrutiny of all pros and cons involved in the action programme.

7. Monitoring must be an in-built feature of the programme in order to avoid any mishap. Attempt should be made to stabilise various interest groups and people's organisations.

Further, Bajpai is very critical of the role of NGO's. He has gone to the extent of saying that funds to NGOs should be stopped. Instead Panchayat Raj institutions should be strengthened further for development intervention through the process of people's participation. He is of the opinion that a critical enabling programme must be launched through a well conceived social education programme throughout in order to really empower the people. He concludes this highly critical piece of writing on people's participation by saying : "Government must understand that conscientation of the people and their active participation in the development process, on one hand, and asserting their rights on the other, does not weaken the authority of the state but is the symptom of true and mature democracy where liberty of thought, expression, belief in faith and worship and equality of status and opportunity that are granted by the constitution itself" (Bajpai, 1998 : 823).

On the basis of the above discussion on the concept of people's participation in development, following specific objectives are pursued in the present study.

1. To assess whether People's Campaign for Decentralised Planning (PCDP) could achieve the declared objectives of the programme such as.

(a) addressing the developmental challenges that Kerala has been confronting for the past two decades.

(b) ushering in a new development culture where there is no difference of opinion among the two major political fronts in the state.

(c) ensuring participation of stake holders in development work by entering into a new development compact.

(d) constructing a bulwark of the masses to resist effectively the onslaught of unbridled globalization.

2. To ascertain why CPI(M) wanted that 9th Plan should be a people's plan.

3. To analyse the impact of power rivalry between the two political coalitions—Left Democratic Front (LDF) and the United Democratic Front (UDF) on democratic decentralisation in Kerala.

4. To examine the differences between the perceptions of the two political coalitions over the issues of democratic decentralisations.

5. To assess the strengths and weaknesses of the institutional set up erected by the State Planning Board for operationalising the mass movement of participatory planning.

6. To examine the level of participation of women, SCs and STs and organised and unorganised sections of population in the grassroots democratic process.

7. To study the attitude of bureaucracy towards decentralised planning with people's participation.

8. To reconstruct the existing theory of people's participation in Development.

Universe of the Study

The universe of the study is the state of Kerala, particularly the programme of people's participation in development planning launched by the State Planning Board. However, it is not physically possible to cover the entire length and breadth of the state for a small study of this type. Therefore, we have concentrated on two Panchayats in the district of Thiruvananthapuram to understand the nature of PCDP. For getting an understanding of the Gram Sabha the Panchayats in Nedumangad Block had been selected.

Data Collection

The study used both primary and secondary data.

The primary data required for the study were generated through interview method. PR and Nagarpalika leadership, samples of low and middle level bureaucracy, Key Resources Persons (KRP), District Level Resource Persons (DRP) and Local Level Resource Persons (LRP) were interviewed with separate sets of interview guides. Besides, discussions were organised among various interest groups to bring out clearly the nature of socio-political processes and structures in the Panchayat identified for the study. In addition to that a survey had been conducted among a sample of hundred people from each Gram Panchayat to obtain their perception about PCDP.

Panchayat developmental reports prepared by a special team of volunteers, people's representatives, bureaucrats and technocrats, data collected from various offices of the line departments, Taluk and Block level offices of various State Government Departments, census reports, studies at Panchayat levels undertaken by various agencies and institutions and archival materials formed the secondary source materials. Study materials pertaining to PCDP and other publications of the Planning Board were also consulted.

Chapter Design

The study is divided into five chapters. First chapter discusses various aspects of the concept of people's participation. Second chapter is an overview of people's campaign for decentralised planning. Third chapter is a report on decentralised planning based on extensive field studies at two of Kerala's Grama Panchayats. The political process at the grassroots level is the theme of the fourth chapter. In the fifth chapter the author arrives at certain conclusions based on the analysis presented in the preceding chapters.

2

PEOPLE'S CAMPAIGN FOR DECENTRALISED PLANNING

An Overview

The Communist Party of India (Marxist) led Left Democratic Front (LDF) government in Kerala decided in July 1996 to devolve 35-40 per cent of the Ninth Five Year Plan Fund to Local Self-Government Institutions (LSGIs) to implement development projects that were drawn up by these bodies with the participation of people at the local level. This unprecedented decision of the state government was based on the recommendations of the first ever meeting of the newly constituted State Planning Board, on 14 July, 1996. The Marxist controlled new Planning Board decided to launch a massive campaign to enlist people's participation. The campaign was formally inaugurated on 17 August, 1996. The State Planning Board had erected a campaign structure to facilitate the campaign and to attract people towards the proposed decentralised planning process. In this chapter we will have a look at the background in which the idea was mooted, its various phases and the mechanism evolved by the Planning Board to carryout the decentralised planning in the State.

Evolution of the Political Vision of the Campaign

The political vision of the campaign emerged out of several contributory factors, the core of which is the Marxist approach to decentralisation that was designed by late E.M.S. Namboodiripad, the CPI(M) veteran of Kerala. T.M Thomas Isaac, the principal protagonist of the campaign, explained the political vision of the campaign by drawing heavily from the writings of E.M.S. Namboodiripad.

Thomas Isaac argues that even though democratic centralism is the organisational principle of CPI(M) it has immense faith in democratic decentralisation as a principle of governance. He explains this point by quoting the example of CPI(M) in West Bengal where that party had implemented a radical decentralisation programme. Why a party whose organisational principle is democratic centralisation should promote democratic decentralisation in the governance of the country? The answer to this question according to Isaac lies in the dissent note that EMS wrote to the Ashok Metha Committee Report on Panchayat Raj Institutions:

> It is from this view point of the organised struggle to end the system of exploitation (Pre-capitalist as well as capitalist) that I am looking at the entire problem of defending and extending democracy.
>
> By democracy here, I mean the system of parliamentary democracy with adult suffrage; periodical elections; elected legislature; the rule of law; full protection of citizens rights and freedoms which are known in our Constitution as the fundamental rights of citizenship, etc. These constitute a set of valuable rights which our working people won after decades of struggle and which can be used by the exploited majority in its struggle against the exploiting minority.
>
> Our experience of working of this system proves that since the parliamentary democratic system as prevails today provides the exploited majority a powerful weapon with which to fight the exploiting minority, the latter does its utmost to reduce democracy to a mere formality to subvert it whenever and wherever the exploited majority uses it to get anywhere near the seats of power. Defence of parliamentary democracy at the central and state level (where it exists but is very often threatened by the authoritarian forces) and its extension to the districts and lower levels as envisaged in the four-pillar democracy is, therefore, of extreme importance in the advance of Indian society.

> My faith in democratic decentralization in other words arises from the fact that it helps the working people in their day-to-day struggles against their oppressors and exploiters (as cited by Thomas Isaac, 2000: 36).

Thomas Isaac reads two dimensions in what is considered as the comprehensive vision on decentralisation as articulated by EMS. The first dimension is that EMS does not distinguish between development and regulatory functions. Secondly, there cannot be full-fledged decentralisation without restructuring of centre-state relations in favour of the latter (*Ibid.*). Thomas Isaac then presents briefly the history of Communist's engagement with local bodies in Kerala ever since they won the Malabar District Board elections in 1952.

The Administrative Reforms Committee (1958) under the Chairmanship of EMS suggested a two-tier local government set up with Panchayats and Municipalities at the grassroots level and District Councils at the district level. The District Council Bill was introduced in the Kerala State Assembly in 1958. But the Bill could not get passed because the EMS Government was dismissed by the Central Government and the Assembly was dissolved in 1959. In 1967 the second EMS Government wanted to enact the two-tier local government set up. The Kerala Panchayat Raj Bill was introduced in 1967. The Government resigned in 1969 and the Bill lapsed. A Kerala District Administration Bill was passed by the Congress Government headed by A.K. Antony in 1979 which was originally introduced in 1971 and re-introduced in 1978 but no attempt was made to implement it till 1987. The LDF Government of Marxist Leader E.K. Nayanar (1987-91) took measures to implement the Act. Elections to District Councils were held in February 1990. In the next Assembly Elections the LDF lost power and a UDF Government under the leadership of Congress leader Karunakaran came to power. The UDF Government of Karunakaran took back all the functions and powers transferred to the District Council in the very first decision of the new government.

It is at this juncture that the Central Government came out with the 73rd and 74th Amendments to the Constitution of India to have uniform pattern of local bodies all over India and to provide constitutional status to them.

While describing the history of Panchayat Raj legislations in Kerala, Thomas Isaac argues that the undivided communist party and later the CPI(M) took measures for democratic decentralisation in Kerala and the Congress and its allies always thwarted all attempts at genuine decentralisation in Kerala. He writes that "our brief survey of the history of decentralisation in Kerala reveals how several Congress governments frustrated the efforts made by the Left government in 1957, 1967 and 1987 (Isaac and Frankie, 2000: 40). The leftists in Kerala always believed that the Congress party paid only lip service to democratic decentralisation. Even though the left in general and the CPM in particular interested in genuine decentralisation their attempts were always frustrated by the Congress due to an inherent weakness of CPM in Kerala. In Isaac's own words :

> ".....unlike the Left Front in West Bengal, the Left Democratic Front in Kerala has not been in power continuously for a long period. Moreover the strength of the CPI(M) within the Left Front has also not been as decisive in terms of Assembly seats. The CPI(M) has had only around half the LDF seats even though the CPI-M's share of voter support within the front is around 80 per cent. The formal vote share of CPI(M) in the total vote secured by the LDF has exhibited a clear trend of decline over time, even though by all indicators its mass strength has improved during the last decades and the mass support of some of the LDF partners generally declines" (*ibid.*).

In addition to the above limitation of CPI(M), the other important impediments to decentralisation in Kerala are "excessive departmentalism and bureaucratic vested interests" (*ibid.*). To substantiate this point Isaac quotes again from the writings of EMS: "There is no doubt that the enemies of decentralisation (the bureaucrats) who have been enjoying the sweet benefits of centralization in the government secretariat would employ every tactic to see that as little as possible is passed down (*ibid.*).

How to break these barriers to decentralisation? Generating political will for creating necessary condition for decentralisation is very difficult.

> "It is in this context that mass mobilization in support of decentralisation reforms becomes important. Only through mobilising the masses and creating a powerful public opinion in favour of decentralisation can the hurdles be overcome" (*ibid.*).

New Development Culture

In 1989 EMS published a pamphlet entitled *Politics of Development* in which he talked about the need for a new political culture in the state. The idea is that the constituent parties of the two political fronts in Kerala should cooperate in the areas of common interest particularly the development of the state without compromising their separate identity.

EMS argued for a new political culture in the state, based on the political reality in the state. Ever since the dismissal of the first communist government in 1959 the politics of the state has been polarised into two more or less equal fronts, the communist front and the anti-communist front led by the Congress. The electoral support of both the fronts is more or less the same and power is alternated between these fronts after every general election. EMS felt this bi-party pattern of coalition increasingly affected developmental activities in the state. Therefore EMS appealed to all political formations in the state to put aside their differences for the development of the state. He argued that all the political parties in the state should make a self-assessment of their positions and start a dialogue on cooperation for the comprehensive development of the state. In this context EMS self critically admitted:

> "I don't claim that the approach of the workers and peasant organisations and political parties leading them are above fault. While they struggle for their rights and demands they have to realize the importance of improving production and productivity in agriculture and industry. Mass organisations of workers and peasants and other

> sections of people and political parties giving leadership to them have to come forward to increase production in the public and private sectors and help to mobilize capital for social investment. I want to publicly state our commitment to rectify mistakes, if any, in this respect from our side (EMS 1991 as quoted by Isaac, 2000:45).

EMS made this self criticism in the context of the empirical findings by a CDS economist in 1991 that the rate of growth of wages was higher than the rate of growth of productivity in the state.

Marxist In-house Dialogue

The attitude of the Congress towards the development debate initiated by EMS was lukewarm. Even then the Marxists continued the debate in their own platforms. A Round Table was organised under the auspices of the theoretical Journal of CPI(M) in Kerala, in which left political party leaders and academics were invited to participate. The theme paper for discussion was written by Thomas Isaac and E.M. Sreedharan. The discussion document summarized and put together the existing ideas on the development and placed it in the party platform for further debate and action.

1. The Kerala model of development with its social sector achievements was the starting point of the paper. The paper opened with what is now regarded as the most famous statement about Kerala—a table comparing its infant mortality, literacy, life expectancy, and birth rate with the rest of India and with the USA along with their respective per capita incomes. India overall presents a typical picture for an under developed country: *low per capita income and low social indicators*. Even at a low level of income,......, Kerala has been successful in meeting the basic needs of its people. The experience of Kerala shows that the people of India do not have to wait indefinitely for the trickle down effect of economic growth to fulfil their basic needs.

2. Kerala's achievements have resulted from re-distributive strategies that have been fashioned in response to mass pressure from below. The struggle of the left has not been only for land reforms and wage increases, but also for the right to shelter,

education, health care, safe drinking water and other basic needs. The Left in Kerala carried forward the progressive legacy of earlier social reform movements. Kerala's experience proves that in an economy like India's where large sectors of the economy still lack clear wage labour relations, the slogan of basic needs can act as a powerful stimulus for mass mobilisation.

3. The social sector achievements did not have a complementary positive impact on economic growth. Despite land reforms there was no remarkable improvement in agricultural productivity. Despite educational expansion, industrial modernisation and diversification remained retarded. As a result unemployment was three times the national average. The quality of the social infrastructure was also deteriorating. The fiscal crisis of the state was rendering it incapable of intervening in the crisis. It had become evident that in the absence of economic growth it would not be possible to sustain re-distribution policies or the welfare gain of the past.

4. The reason for the crisis lay in historical specificities of the capitalist path of development of the region and in the national and global crisis of capitalism. But given the uneven development of the left movement in India, in regions such as Kerala where the movement is more advanced, it is important to attempt to find partial solutions to some of the most pressing problems in a democratic and pro-people manner. The possibilities for an autonomous development path are foreclosed by the national economic reforms. Given the specific situation in Kerala, a conscious intervention for a re-direction of development policy became imperative.

5. The economic stagnation had serious political implications. It was giving rise to a number of divisive tendencies: unemployment provided a fertile ground for caste-based movements for and against reservation policies. Right wing ideologies were attacking the left ever more successfully. The Left, they argued, had no programme for increasing production. The stagnation, they said, resulted from the redistribution policies the Left had been pushing. Market rigidities introduced by the Left were the cause of Kerala's failure to achieve its growth potential. Even many liberals, who otherwise prided themselves in Kerala's re-distribution programmes,

seemed to be veering towards the position that the Left had fulfilled its historic role in bringing about more equitable distribution. Now it should make way for market forces in order to achieve rapid growth. In the new global environment these ideas became fashionable in Kerala. But was there a democratic alternative?

6. Given the class structure of the region characterized by petty production units, but with a high incidence of wage labour, improving productivity has become a necessary condition for achieving the units of petty producers and wage labourers. In this manner improvement in production assumes special importance in ensuring class unity and in furthering the class struggle. Defending the public infrastructure in education, health and other sectors is no longer possible without improving the quality of their services. All these necessitate a reorientation of the mass movements towards direct intervention in the development process in order to improve productivity or improve the quality of services.

7. Decentralisation is necessary to provide an organisational framework for participatory development in the petty production and social service sectors. It was also important to overhaul the institutional arrangements for land and water management, provision of social services and the cooperatives.

8. The paper did not attempt to spell out specific policies for each sector but emphasised the need for a critical evaluation of the development policies being pursued in Kerala. Old dogmatic positions that romanticised large scale canal irrigation, clear cutting forests for plantations, and massive harvesting of fishing resources, had to be revised. In health and education quantitative expansion was not needed as much as quality improvement. Greater emphasis on the productive sectors was needed along with solutions to the crisis in infrastructure, particularly the lack of adequate electrical power (Isaac, 2000).

Thomas Isaac writes that EMS endorsed the basic proposition put forward and at the same time expressed serious reservations about the concept of a Kerala model of development as described by some western observers because it distracted attention from the urgency of accelerating economic growth. EMS sharply focused on this issue:

> Kerala faces today an intense economic crisis in production agricultural and industrial. I am inclined to believe that while we have spent much time and attention on "social sector" issues of welfare and improvement of the living standards of the people we have not paid enough attention to or shown adequate concern for pressing problems of economic growth and material production. I make a request: let not the praise that scholars shower on Kerala for its achievements divert attention from the intense economic crisis that we face. We are behind other states of India in respect of economic growth and a solution to this crisis brooks no delay. We can ignore our backwardness in respect of employment and production only at our own peril (Namboodiripad 1994 as cited in Isaac, 2000:44).

Based on this thinking of EMS an International Congress on Kerala studies was organised in August 1994 under the auspices of A.K.G. Centre for Research and Studies. This multi-disciplinary Congress was a big event. Participants from all the states in India and from 23 other countries attended it. 600 papers were presented and discussed. However no formal conclusion was drawn up from the Congress. What were emerged at the end were certain broad perspectives. Differences persisted with regard to solutions but there was a definite gravitation of the dialogue towards the broad development perspective that we have already discussed. Re-orientation of the focus of planning towards strengthening material production and improvement in the quality of services required a thorough overhaul of the sectoral policies that were being followed.While industrialisation and infrastructural development required determined state level intervention, a decentralised development strategy was more suited for petty production sectors and, for basic services" (Isaac, 2000:49). The Marxist strategists consider the International Congress on Kerala studies as "an important landmark in the move towards a broad social consensus on the development of the state". As a result of continuous discussions and debates a coherent strategy with two pillars was evolved by 1996 to address the development crisis of the state. The first pillar is "resolute state intervention" in power sector and inviting private capital in electronics, light engineering and other industries where the state had comparative advantage. The second pillar which is considered as the "centre piece" of the strategy was decentralisation with the involvement of the masses for increasing productivity in small scale sectors and to improve the quality of life in public services. The CPI(M) believed that this kind of a "democratic response to economic crisis" would help to undermine the bi-polar compartmentalisation of Kerala politics. The Marxist leaders further believed that such a strategy would "facilitate further advance of the left in the state".

People's Plan – The Ideological Plane

The activists of People's Campaign for Decentralized Planning (PCDP) desired that all sections of the people should cooperate with it without being affected by sectarian political perspectives and interests. PCDP was projected as a non-political platform where everyone in Kerala could come together for the comprehensive development of the state by strengthening and deepening the contours of democracy. This kind of a formulation about the ideological plane of PCDP is misleading. PCDP has a well thought out ideology. This has been well explained in the writings of EMS, Thomas Isaac and in the publications of the Planning Board on PCDP.

The development perspective of PCDP is rooted in the concept of self-reliance. It is projected as a bulwark against the onslaughts of globalisation in the state. Here emerges the ideology of PCDP that is based on Kerala left's particularly CPI(M)'s, perspective on decentralisation. This concept of decentralisation which we have already discussed is diametrically opposite to the current thinking on development and decentralisation as propagated by World Bank which considers globalisation and decentralisation as complementary tendencies of the new millennium. Activists of

PCDP identify four basic differences between World Bank concept and the leftist view on decentralisation and development.

Firstly, the approach of World Bank is based on the neo-liberal concept of down sizing the state. The ideology of people's plan stands not for down sizing the state but deepening the state through democratisation of the society by way of strengthening local government institutions.

Secondly, weakening of the state through privatisation and marketisation is the ultimate objective of the kind of decentralisation advocated by World Bank. The objective of people's plan is not marketisation but planned development with mass participation. The argument is that everything cannot be left to the market. Instead local requirements can be decided by the local community themselves. This does not mean that PCDP is completely rejecting the market. But it believes in the social control of market.

Thirdly, the World Bank conceptualisation of decentralisation stands for total withdrawal of state from development functions and transferring of these functions to NGOs. This is not the approach of PCDP. The Kerala government has transferred social welfare functions to the local bodies and funds for implementing such programmes have been allocated by the government from its revenues. The state has not withdrawn from development function but only transferred these functions to the local governments.

Fourthly, the World Bank is also talking about participatory development. In World Bank conceptualization, participation is involvement of individuals and NGOs in development work. The objective is to de-politicise civil society and turn it against the state with the larger objective of creating local societies subservient to the interests of globalisation. The World Bank conceived such a strategy to destroy progressive political movements in the Third World. But for the managers of PCDP, participation is not the mere involvement of individuals and NGOs in development activities, it is an attempt to involve class and mass organisations in local democracy and local level development. In short PCDP advocated a local production system and a local market for these locally produced goods and services.

People's Plan: The Context

The State Planning Board had published a number of books and handouts to educate the people about the urgency of people's campaign for decentralised planning and it also issued instructions and guidelines for the volunteers and officials involved in the campaign activities. All these literatures begin by defining the context in which the LDF Government decided to introduce decentralised planning in Kerala with people's participation.

According to the State Planning Board the importance and timeliness of the people's plan campaign should be understood in the light of the following:

(a) The prevailing critique of the centralised planning and administration in the country;
(b) Failure of hitherto efforts at decentralisation and the intimidating long list of obstacles that new attempts at genuine decentralisation face; and
(c) The contemporary development challenges of the state of Kerala, which by consensus demand a decentralised approach to planning as also a revival of the participatory spirit to protect the widely acclaimed gains of the past.

Now let us listen to the elaboration of these points by the people's plan activists and the State Planning Board.

Experience of Centralised Planning

The five-year plans in vogue in India from the early fifties had not been successful in finding solutions to basic problems such as mass poverty and unemployment due to over 'centralisation'. The major hurdle in the way of total development is assessed as the centralised approach to planning. The Planning Board literature says:

> The widespread apathy among people and their lack of involvement in nation building activities, indifference to the development needs of the people and channeling of resources for wrongly perceived goals, total disregard of local specificities even where it matters most, lack of effort at integration of isolated development interventions which often tend to work

at cross purposes, and above all spiraling of corruption may be attributed to the centralized approach of planning that was in force.

At the same time the Planning Board is aware that everything cannot be properly done at the local level. There are issues that are to be addressed at the state or national level. However, the areas in which development intervention can be done at the local level are also part of the centralised planning till now. Therefore, SPB is advocating a system of multi-level planning "where the local unit is allowed to plan and implement everything that can be performed most effectively at that level and all the rest is left to the higher levels". This philosophy of people's plan is succinctly stated in another handout.

Despite the acclaimed advantages of decentralisation of planning and repeated commitments made in its favour, the planning process in India has, so far, remained a highly centralised affair. There has been very little serious effort to develop planning capabilities at lower levels. Even state plans, more often than not, are mere aggregations of departmental schemes trimmed and modified to suit the national framework and targets.

In the above circumstances the LDF Government wanted to make the Ninth Plan a decentralised one with people's participation at the local level with a view to overcome the "departmentalism" of centralised planning.

Obstacles to Genuine Decentralisation

Planning Board had no doubt about the desirability of decentralised planning. According to Planning Board decentralised planning had to be conceptualised in accordance with the ideals of *Gram Swaraj* the roots of which could be traced to the days of freedom movement. In the post-independence period also decentralisation of power continued to enjoy priority in the national agenda for making the country's governance more democratic. Despite the fact of such priority for the process of decentralisation, it failed to take off due to a variety of reasons. Planning Board identified these reasons as:

1. Resistance offered by the vested interests nurtured by the centralised structure;

2. Lack of pressure from below due to the absence of representative governments at levels below the states; and
3. Paucity of expertise and preparedness at the local level.

In the past, there were many efforts to overcome these difficulties and to experiment with genuine process of decentralisation especially in states, like Rajasthan, Karnataka and West Bengal. In various places in India efforts at micro-level interventions were made under the auspices of various NGOs and people's movements. In 1993, the country got a broad framework to attempt at genuine decentralisation in the form of 73rd and 74th Amendments to the Constitution of India. These constitutional amendments provided a favourable framework. The quantum of devolution of power and resource was left with the state legislature. The situation was that the state governments could either make use of the constitutional provisions effectively or just thwart decentralisation by making use of the loopholes in the constitutional amendments mentioned above.

In the context of Kerala, a new government fully committed to genuine decentralisation came into power according to State Planning Board (SPB). The LDF Government was totally committed to a total restructuring of the system. "But this alone is not enough. It has been the experience of the state that the success of government initiatives and legislations depends a lot on the environment in which such movements are made and the pressure exerted from below". Viewed from this angle, the people's plan campaign is "an effort to consolidate and articulate public opinion in favour of decentralised planning and thereby help the government to translate its commitment to concrete actions".

The Development Challenges of Kerala

The people's plan campaign is also a product of a dialogue among the left intellectuals in Kerala about the crisis that was encountered by the much publicized Kerala Model of Development. The state could achieve high quality of life without required level of economic growth. This was due to mass movements and appropriate government intervention in social sectors. However, for the past two decades or so this development model has been under the grip of a severe crisis due to stagnation in the production sectors and quality erosion in the service sectors. Following are the problems in the productive sectors: (i) the virtual stagnation of the agricultural sector, (ii) the deplorably lower level of productivity of important crops, (iii) growing apathy among cultivators, (iv) structural decay of the industrial sector dominated by the ailing traditional industries, (v) rapid deterioration of the power situation, and (vi) over-burdening of the fragile ecosystems, etc.

Other aspects of social life have also been affected by the severe crisis. Massive deterioration was noted in the performance of sectors such as education, public health and transport. Government has become incapable of making effective intervention due to the fiscal crisis as a result of stagnation in productive sectors. The re-distributive gains of the yester years have been severely affected by the development crisis noted above.

This contemporary crisis had led the SPB to the realisation that "the pursuit of equality cannot be sustained in the absence of economic growth" The Board further said that the people's campaign for the Ninth Plan was an initiative to utilise the legacy of collective social intervention to face the contemporary challenge of development.

The Planning Board said that "the decline in the quality of services, especially of those supplied by the public sector needs urgent remedial measure, for it has already started affecting the quality of life of people, especially vulnerable sections of society" Planning Board literature on the subject further said that the over centralised system of development planning and implementation was totally unsuitable to take on these challenges. This is particularly true in the case of land and water management, development of agriculture and allied sectors, rural and cottage industries, drinking water, sanitation and other social service sectors.

Further more, the SPB had found the emergence of a consensus in favour of decentralised system of administration and planning. This, according to SPB, was evident from the popular support received by certain micro-level development experiments taken up by Kerala Sastra Sahitya Parishad (KSSP) and the Total Literacy

Campaign. It was under these circumstances that the Planning Board articulated its idea of people's campaign for Ninth Five Year plan. With this information about the background in which people's campaign was conceived, we would now enlist the objectives of the campaign. In its broad sense PCDP "is an attempt to Conceptualise, Operationalise and Institutionalise a system of multi-level, people centred planning process suitable to the specificities of Kerala. It is also of equal importance to the campaign that the system of multi-level planning thus put in place help the state to overcome its contemporary development crisis".

According to the State Planning Board following are the specific objectives of People's Plan Campaign:

1. Re-constructing the received ideas on decentralisation and people's planning.

2. Enabling the State government to translate its commitment to concrete actions by conscientising and mobilising people in support.

3. Harnessing popular opinion and will to over-come resistance offered by vested interests.

4. Correcting popular and well entrenched but wrong notions of development by initiating development dialogues and introducing plausible alternatives.

5. Imparting knowledge and skills needed for local level planning, involving mass organisations of the people in development activities, inculcating a favourable attitude among officials and technocrats and above all evolving and institutionalising a systematic procedure by which development needs of the people are articulated, suitable solutions are arrived at, projectised, prioritised, integrated into comprehensive development plans, implemented and monitored with maximum people's participation at all levels.

6. Horizontal and vertical integration of planning among various tiers.

7. In addition to the objectives stated above another major objective of the people's campaign was to facilitate further advancement of the left in the state (Isaac, 2000:35).

The campaign cell of the State Planning Board made earnest efforts to bring together and motivate the groups of people mentioned below in every locality for the purpose of drawing upon the Ninth Plan.

First, the elected representatives at the three-tiers of LSGIs: The effort of the SPB was to make the elected representatives aware of their responsibility and to equip them for a hither to unknown style of cooperation and teamwork.

Secondly, Government officials: The attempt of the planning Board was to re-orient government officials to perform planning responsibilities under the direction of the Panchayats and Urban Local bodies.

Thirdly, cooperation of non-officials: The expertise of non-officials in the plan process was to be made available to LSGIs.

Fourthly, the mass of people: So far common man remained as the passive objects of the development process. The attempt was to transform them into active partners, rather than passive objects.

And finally, the mass organizations of people: These organisations were required to be re-oriented to undertake new development initiatives.

In short, PCDP wanted to achieve a major change in the attitude of officials, experts, elected representatives and the people at large. From this the Planning Board experts wanted the creation of a new development culture that would contribute towards narrowing down of rivalries of a sharp nature, the product of highly polarised party politics of the two dominant fronts.

The Various Phases of the Campaign

The campaign wanted to ensure that local self-government institutions in rural areas and urban localities would prepare and prioritize a shelf of integrated schemes, in a scientific and participatory manner, so that programmes for the 9th Plan could be selected from among them on a priority basis. This process of planning from below was initially divided into five phases. Each phase was to be proceeded by a preparatory stage, the most important component of which was the training of resource persons (Voluntary workers, officials and people's representatives) at various levels.

I Phase (October 1996) : Need Identification through People's Assembly (Gram Sabha/Ward Conventions)

The first phase of the campaign was the identification of the needs of the people and the identification of gaps in local level development. In order to achieve this objective special Gram Sabha and ward conventions were convened in Panchayats and Municipalities and Municipal Corporations respectively. The campaign at this stage was oriented towards weaker sections of the society.

1. Ensuring maximum participation of people, especially women and other weaker sections of the society.

2. Guiding the deliberations to identify the needs of the people and find the gaps in local level development.

Around 650 Key Resource Persons (KRP) at the state level, 12,000 resource persons at the district level (DRP) and more than 1,00,000 resource persons at the local level (LRP) were given training to take up active role in conducting the Gram Sabha and group discussions on development sectors, and facilitate structured discussions. In order to ensure maximum participation, the Gram Sabhas and ward conventions were convened on holidays; squads of volunteers visited households and explained the programme. Preparatory meetings of mass organisation were held; and an active propaganda using colourful posters, advertisements and involving all branches of the media was resorted to. It is estimated that around 30 lakh people participated in the Gram Sabha and ward conventions specially convened during September-October 1996. As expected during the course of this phase local people who attended the Gram Sabha/ward conventions identified development problems of their locality.

II Phase (November-December 1996) : Situation Analysis and Strategy Setting

Development seminars at Panchayat and Municipal levels were the most important event during this phase. Development seminars were organised with a view to suggest solutions to the development problems identified by the Gram Sabha/ward convention. A printed report on the socio-economic status of the Local body was made available to the participants of the development seminar to facilitate sectorwise discussions. The development reports were prepared on the following basis:

1. Consolidation of Gramsabha/ward convention reports.
2. Review of ongoing schemes.
3. Collection of secondary data.
4. Geographical study of the area.
5. A brief survey of local history.

An objective assessment of the natural and human resources and the related development problem was made through systematic secondary data collection; rapid appraisal techniques such as transect walks and semi-official reviews of on going programmes. The preparations of development report were a logical culmination of above activities.

The II Phase has the following output:

(a) Generation of an extensive local data base.
(b) A comprehensive survey of all development sectors for all Panchayats and Municipalities.
(c) A list of plausible solutions.
(d) Formation of task forces to prepare development projects for each development sector.

In short, the situation analysis phase constituted detailed data gathering at the Gram Panchayat/Municipality level and drawing up inferences after analysis. Based on the people's perceptions of their requirements and based on the problems and prospects emerging out of the analysis of data, development seminars were held resulting in the identification of key areas for local level development.

III Phase (January-March 1997) : Task Forces and Projectisation

The Development seminars at the Panchayat and Municipal levels only arrived at broad statements of solutions to various development problems. The third phase of the campaign sought to convert these solutions into project/scheme proposals in a format that could be included in the plan. The task forces formed at the development seminars in 13 key development areas like health, education, agriculture, etc. prepared project proposals based on the Development Reports. As many as 12,000 taskforces functioned at the village level alone with a total participation of at least 1.2 lakh persons in the whole of the state. The task forces prepared around one-lakh projects for the consideration of the Panchayats.

The task of preparation demanded participation of more officials and technically qualified people than the earlier phases. Accordingly, special efforts were made to assure participation of officials and local level experts. While chairperson of the task force was an elected representative, an officer from the concerned line department was supposed to be its convener.

An elected member headed the task forces constituted in each Gram Sabha/ward committee with an officer as convener and NGO activists, officials and local volunteers as members.

In order to ensure uniformity, it was suggested that the project reports should generally have the following components :

1. *Introduction*: explaining necessity and relevance of the project.

2. *Objectives*: in well defined (as far as possible in quantitative/ measurable) terms.

3. *Beneficiaries*: Criteria proposed to be followed in selecting beneficiaries or benefiting areas.

4. *Activities*: technical analysis and time frame of all project activities.

5. *Organisations and Agencies:* their role in implementing the project activities.

6. *Financial analysis*: investment needed for each activity and identification of source of funds.

7. *Cost-Benefit Analysis*: Preliminary analysis of all direct and indirect benefits and costs including a gender and environment impact statement.

8. *Monitoring*: Details of the proposed monitoring mechanism.

The Planning Board issued a set of guidelines for the preparation of Special Component Plan (SCP) and Tribal Sub-Plan (TSP) projects. Further, it was recommended that the local bodies earmark 10 per cent of the plan assistance for projects meant for development of women. Special care was taken to see that the task forces prepare projects with an integrated approach.

IV Phase (March-April 1997) : Draft Plan of Grassroots Tiers

During the fourth phase, the projects prepared by the task forces were to be prioritized and incorporated into the five year plans of the Panchayat. For finalising the plan, the Panchayats had to:

* make a clear assessment of their capacity to mobilise resources from various sources to finance the plan.
* evolve a development strategy on the basis of problems identified and resource potential of the locality, prioritize and select projects to implemented; and
* decide on a monitoring mechanism for successful implementation of each project selected.

The Panchayats had been asked to earmark at least 40 to 50 per cent for productive sector (Agriculture, Animal Husbandry, Fisheries, Small Industries), 30 to 40 per cent for social sector (Health, Education, Water Supply, Sanitation etc.) and 10 to 30 per cent for infrastructure (Roads, etc.).

V Phase (March-April 1997) : Formulation of Plans of Higher Tiers

During this phase the Block and District Panchayats prepared their plan documents. Block and District plans had to integrate local level plans and design complementary programmes.

VI Phase (April 1997): Voluntary Technical Corps—Appraisal and Approval of Plans

The main task of this phase was to examine the technical feasibility, financial viability and social acceptability of the projects included in the plans of the local bodies. This was required to be done by a competent authority so that necessary technical and other sanctions might be easily obtained for the projects thus approved.

Around 1.5 lakh projects had to be evaluated. It was stated that the evaluation was not for selection or rejection but to actually correct and finalise the projects. The projects were divided into two categories:

1. Projects those are included in the annual plan 1997-98.
2. Projects for subsequent years. The SPB mobilized technical experts, mostly retired professionals and officials to voluntarily take up the jobs. The Voluntary Technical Corps (VTC) vetted the plans.

VII Phase : Release of First Instalment of Plan Assistance

The plan was finalized once District Planning Committee (DPC) approved the Panchayat plan with the comments of Voluntary Technical Corps (VTC). Thereafter the first instalment of plan assistance was given to LSGIs.

The Procedure Prescribed for the Selection of Beneficiaries for Rural Local/Bodies

With the decentralisation of powers and functions the selection of beneficiaries in most of the schemes was made the responsibility of local bodies. In the case of rural areas, the Gram Panchayats were to select the beneficiaries and in urban areas, the Municipalities or the Municipal Corporations as the case might be.

For that purpose a transparent procedure had been prescribed. The details of the procedure for the identification of the beneficiaries are described below:

In the case of Panchayat Raj institutions, basically the Gram Sabhas were entrusted with the responsibilities of identifying the beneficiaries. Since the District Panchayats and Block Panchayats could not convene the Gram Sabha, they got the beneficiary selected through the respective Gram Panchayats.

The gram Panchayats carried out selection process through the Gram Sabha and submitted the selection list to the Block and District Panchayats for approval. This meant that the number of beneficiaries to be selected by each Gram Panchayat would have to be determined in advance by the District and Block Panchayats. For determining this number the District and Block Panchayats had first laid down objective criteria for selecting the target groups. These criteria were related to the type of scheme. In the case of beneficiaries to be selected for schemes implemented by the Gram Panchayat, the priority list for each ward for a particular scheme was prepared by the Gram Sabha and selection at the Panchayat level based on the criteria for eligibility and prioritization. It was instructed that there should not be any ward-wise targets and eligibility would be considered at the level of the Gram Panchayat keeping in view the priority list prepared by the Gram Sabha. However, Panchayat might, if necessary, determine the upper ceiling of nominations to be prioritized exceeded twice the target for the Gram Panchayat as a whole. From the priority list the selection had to be made based on specific criteria of prioritization which were laid down in advance. Priority fixed by Gram Sabha could not normally be changed for that area.

Determination of Criteria

In the case of centrally and state sponsored schemes, eligibility criteria prescribed by those scheme guidelines had to be followed. In the case of schemes/projects planned for the different tiers of Panchayat, the eligibility criteria were determined by that Panchayat as stated in the project approved by the District Planning Committee. The Panchayat at each level were asked to state clearly in writing the prioritization criteria that were followed to short list eligible beneficiaries in cases where all the eligible beneficiaries could not be considered under the scheme. While applying the prioritization criteria the Gram Sabha could fine tune them going into greater detail within each criterion if required.

Publicity

The Panchayats were instructed to give widespread publicity to the criteria adopted both for eligibility and for prioritization. The guideline prescribed that publicity should be given through elected persons, resource persons of the planning campaign, political parties and their affiliated organisations, voluntary organisations, field staff, etc. A notice clearly indicating the number of schemes, the criteria for each scheme and the number of beneficiaries selected were to be displayed at the Panchayat office, Village office and concerned office and other prominent places. A separate Notice Board was to be set up in each ward for this purpose. Pamphlets might also be printed and circulated. Press releases could also be made.

Application Form

For all schemes application forms were to be designed in Malayalam or local language. The application form should be simple but should contain provisions for incorporating all required details needed for applying the eligibility as well as prioritization criteria. The application form should state these criteria in its Annexure. The application forms were to be distributed for a fixed period preceding the Gram Sabha and at the Gram Sabha. A common application form for group of similar schemes could be prepared.

Verification

The application form contained in it a proforma verification form. The Gram Panchayat was asked to decide on a system of verification either through designated officers or designated sub-committee. Three types of verifications were thought of. Initially as many application as possible were enquired into using the arrangements made by the Panchayat. Then, the applications for which verification was not completed and the application which was received on the spot were enquired into on the spot in the Gram Sabha by the chairperson of the sub-group and the official nominated for this purpose by the Gram Panchayat. In case factual details were not available during the meeting of the Gram Sabha, the same arrangements made for verification earlier continued and verified the facts. In such cases the priority list was prepared by the Gram Sabha subject to the verification report and this was made clear in the Gram Sabha.

Gram Sabha Meetings

Gram Sabha meetings were to be called immediately thereafter. Application forms were to be distributed at the beginning of the Gram Sabha also. Then the list of applicants from the applications received earlier and on the spot was to be drawn up. The eligibility criteria and prioritization criteria should be explained to the Gram Sabha. Thereafter the Gram Sabha could break-up into groups for various sectors and in the sectoral groups the prioritization of the applicants could be made. In addition to the criteria decided by the Panchayat, sub-criteria for prioritization to match the local perceptions of eligibility could be made. All the applications vetted according to the criteria and the priority list prepared by consensus. If there was no rational method of discrimination then lots could be drawn if agreed by everybody. Wherever neighbourhood groups exist Panchayats utilised their services for vetting the eligibility of a beneficiary.

In the case of beneficiary oriented scheme under Tribal Sub-Plan, selection should not be made in the general Gram Sabha. Special Gram Sabha consisting of all the tribal families in the ward would be called and selection made by this general body and tribal families from all the tribal settlements in the ward.

Actual Selection of beneficiaries

With the prioritized list from each ward, after completing verification of facts, a list based on clear criteria of prioritization should be drawn up for the Gram Panchayat as a whole. This should be drawn up in the Gram Panchayat committee meeting. In that special meeting the local press and the public were given access.

Once Gram Panchayat finalized the list it published it as a draft in the order of priority and indicating the factors which resulted in the priority rank in a tabular form. If any objections received on the draft list, Gram Panchayat considered it after further verification if required and recorded its views on accepting or rejecting it. Thereafter the final list was published. In the case of Block Panchayat and District Panchayat, Gram Panchayats should send the final list to them with all the applications and documents related to the selection for taking the final decision. The lists submitted by the Gram Panchayats should be published as drafts by the district and Block Panchayats calling for objections, if any. This should be published simultaneously in the District or Block Panchayats and the concerned Gram Panchayat. Only after clearing the objections should the list was finalized.

Transparency

All the documents like application forms, verification reports, enquiry reports and decision minutes are public documents which everyone has access and copies of which everyone can procure. In the next Gram Sabha meeting after the selection the selected Gram Sabha list concerning that Gram Sabha might be given with adequate justifications. Comments by Gram Sabha may be recorded. If it is proved later that the beneficiary or the enquiring officer or the selecting authority is responsible for an ineligible selection, such person or persons shall be liable to reimburse the expenses with interest.

Procedure Prescribed for the Selection of Beneficiaries in Urban Local Bodies

In the case of Municipalities and Municipal Corporations, the procedure prescribed in the case of PRIs would *mutatis mutandis* apply. In the place of Gram Sabhas, ward committees would perform the function. In the urban areas the close contacts and homogeneity normally seen in rural areas might not be there. Therefore, the application for various schemes should be called in advance after giving much publicity as suggested earlier. The ward committees, the CDS structures and residents associations should be given advance intimation of the selection of beneficiaries. Press release should also be invariably made.

After receipts of all the applications, a detailed verification had to be done of the facts mentioned in the application. Based on this verification report and on the eligibility and prioritization criteria, the ward committee should prepare a priority list. The ceiling of nominations for each ward committee under each scheme must be prescribed by the municipal body. In the case of anti-poverty programmes the specific recommendations of the Area Development Societies (ADS) should be obtained and placed before the ward committee. In the ward committee meeting all the eligible applicants should be called and prioritization done in their presence based on the prioritization criteria applying the facts revealed in the verification process. Here again all the records are deemed to be public documents.

The procedures described above can properly ensure people's participation in the identification and selection of beneficiaries for various schemes. If these criteria and norms are strictly adhered to in a transparent manner, there is absolutely no scope for discretion or patronage, claimed the Planning Board.

Execution of Public Works

Execution of public works is a gold mine of the perpetrators of corruption. It is not a secret that thirty to forty percentages of the development funds invariably go to the pockets of administrative officials, engineers and contractors. A portion of what has been pocketed by bureaucracy, technocracy and contractors comes to the politician in the form of contribution to party fund and election fund. As part of the participatory planning process the Government of Kerala issued a number of rules and regulations that intended to control siphoning off development funds. Among these the most important are the following :

(a) Beneficiary committees and workers cooperatives should be given preference to private contractors in the execution of public works.

(b) All the details of public works being executed should be prominently displayed at the work site.

(c) Social audit committees of Gram Sabha/ward committee can inspect the work and the documents related to it.

It is an open secret that the engineers used to take commission at the time of measurements and check measurements and the bureaucracy at the time of providing advances and final settlement of bills. New rules and regulations have been issued by the government as desired by the Planning Board, in the matter of cost estimation, technical sanction and administrative sanction of projects, fixing up of market rates for the purchase of materials, land acquisition, etc. with a view to ensure total transparency in construction works. Besides, it was expected that the social audit system that the people's plan campaign had incorporated could control effectively the menace of corruption at the time of measurements and passing of bills.

Monitoring Team

A monitoring team has been constituted to assess the progress in the implementation of the project and to ensure quality in work executed. Representatives of the Gram Panchayat Samiti, beneficiary committee and technical exerts were included in the monitoring team. It is prescribed that there should be at least five members in the team. The members of the team have been selected by the Gram Panchayat Samiti and the beneficiary committee. Monitoring team is entitled to examine the execution of the project. If the team found that the work was not satisfactory it was given the power to ask the engineer/contractor/convener to take corrective measures. Monitoring is not an evaluation after the completion of the project. It is a kind of people's supervision of public works.

Audit

Performance Audit

A performance audit system has been introduced in addition to the statutory audit of local bodies. This is a running audit which is more corrective and helpful than fault finding in order to achieve the objective of detecting problems as and when they crop up. The government established a performance audit authority with local administration secretary as state performance audit authority. District level units for Gram Panchayats, Block Panchayats and Regional level units for District Panchayats, Municipalities and Corporations have been established. The performance audit system would conduct performance audit once in a quarter in each local body.

Statutory Audit

As per the provisions of Sections 215(3) and 295(3) of Kerala Panchayat Raj Act and Municipality Act respectively a statutory audit should be conducted annually by the Local Fund Audit Department. The audit party of the Local Fund Audit Department is entitled to visit any local body at any time in the year with or without prior information. They can examine all the records of the local body. Apart from this there shall be an audit by the Accountant General.

Social Audit

In addition to performance audit, statutory audit and AG's audit there shall be a unique social audit by the Gram Sabha/ward committee. For this purpose the Gram Sabha/ward committee is empowered to get all the relevant details of project implementation. Gram Sabha, if it deems necessary, can examine the records, reports and other details of project implementation. Gram Panchayat Samiti can work out the modalities of social audit.

Independent Grievance Redressal System—Ombudsman

The government established an independent grievance redressal system exclusively for the local bodies, by name Ombudsman. Before setting up of Ombudsman, the government, as an interim measure, established a grievance enquiry committee at the district and state levels to enquire into complaints regarding non-adherence to rules and procedures in the implementation of various development schemes by the local bodies.

The district level committee consisted of the District Collector, the senior most non-members of the District level expert committee and the District Planning Officer. This committee was authorized to receive complaints concerning Gram Panchayats, Block Panchayats and Municipalities. The State Level Committee consisted of Secretary, Local Administration, Secretary Planning and Member, Decentralised Planning, State Planning Board. This committee was authorised to receive complaints concerning District Panchayats and Municipal Corporations.

Both the committees were empowered to enquire into complaints using any method deemed appropriate by the committee and shall as far as practicable, sort out issues through consultation and discussions. Wherever statutory action was required these committees intimated the government. This interim setup came to an end with the establishment of Ombudsman. The LDF Government constituted a seven member Ombudsman in which a retired High Court Judge and Senior bureaucrats were made members. The seven members Ombudsman Committee of the LDF government was disbanded by the UDF Government immediately after coming into power and reconstituted the Ombudsman structure with a single member.

Technical Audit Panel

A Technical Audit Panel had also been constituted consisting of not more than 15 senior engineering professionals both governmental and non-governmental. The professionals were identified jointly by planning and local administration departments. The members of this panel might be sent individually or in teams to check implementation of public works or to verify complaints. During inspections these experts could look into the observance of the provisions of public works rules and the governmental instructions issued thereunder with particular reference to the quality of work, ensuring of transparency and avoidance of *benami* (spurious) contractors.

Administrative Reforms

Along with the decision to launch a campaign for involving common man in the decentralised planning process, the LDF Government appointed a Committee on Decentralisation of Powers in July 1996 headed by Satya Brata Sen of West Bengal. The Committee was asked to make recommendations to amend the existing Kerala Panchayat Raj Act enacted by the UDF government as the conformity legislations to the 73rd and 74th Amendments to the Indian Constitution. The Committee was also asked to suggest administrative reform measures to make decentralisation more effective. The Sen Committee submitted its interim report in August 1996 and the final report in 1997. The recommendations of the Sen Committee were accepted and the Kerala Panchayat Raj Act, 1994 and the Municipality Act, 1994 were amended accordingly in 1999. Before coming to these amendments we must have a look at the salient features of the 73rd and 74th Amendments to the Constitution of India and the drawbacks of Kerala Act, 1994 as identified by the LDF government. The highlights of the 73rd and 74th Amendments are given below:

1. These two amendments have constitutionalised Local Self Government Institutions in India.

2. Rural Local Bodies (Panchayats) and Urban Local Bodies (Nagarpalikas) could be entrusted with the responsibility of (a) preparing plans for economic development and social justice, and (b) implementation of schemes for economic development and social justice.

3. Incorporated 11th and 12th schedules to the Constitution of India to distribute powers between the state legislatures on the one hand and Panchayats and Municipalities on the other just as the 7th schedule which distributes powers between the Indian Union and the constituent states.

4. A three-tier system of Panchayats—village, intermediate and district levels—uniformly all over India is mandated (the states whose population is not exceeding 20 lakhs, need not constitute the intermediate Panchayat).

5. A Village Assembly (Gram Sabha) in each village or group of villages.

6. Direct election to all seats in the LSGIs at all levels.

7. Direct or indirect election to the office of Chairperson of village Panchayat; indirect election to such offices of the intermediate and District Panchayats (election from among the elected members).

8. Reservation of seats for Scheduled Castes and Scheduled Tribes in proportion to their population in the Panchayat; reservation of not less than one-third of such reserved seats to the women belonging to the SCs and STs.

9. Reservation of not less than one-third of total number of seats for women.

10. Reservation of office of Chairpersons at all levels of Panchayats to SC and ST in proportion to their population in the state; reservation of not less than one-third of offices of Chairpersons for women.

11. Reservation of seats and offices of chairpersons will be in rotation.

12. A uniform term of five years for the elected bodies in the event of supercession re-elections within six months.

13. State legislature may authorise the Panchayat to levy local taxes and direct the state governments to make grants-in-aid to the Panchayat from the Consolidated Fund.

14. A State Finance Commission should be set up in every five years to review financial position of local bodies and to make suitable recommendations on the distribution of funds between state and the local bodies.

15. A State Election Commission to prepare electoral rolls and to conduct elections.

16. A District Planning Committee to prepare district plans integrating the Plans of the rural and urban local bodies.The Constitutional amendments comprising above features were enacted by the Indian Parliament unanimously and which came into force on 24th April, 1993. The initial attitude of the State Governments towards these amendments was not encouraging. However, all the states have come out with their conformity Acts subsequently. Though these two amendments to the Constitution of India are considered as revolutionary by the enthusiasts of democratic decentralisation they are not free from criticisms. The Kerala leftists' criticism is given below:

The main objection is that the amendments do not envisage any devolution of powers or transfer of schemes from the centre to the states or the lower governments are not considered as the third tiers of the administrative system in the country. Even many of the rural development schemes are controlled and monitored by the

Centre. The Constitutional Amendments do not make the devolution of powers and transfer of functions of the State government to the local governments mandatory.

In many States, the empowerment of Panchayat Raj Institutions is therefore nominal. Though the Constitutional Amendments speak of Gram Sabhas as the elector's body in the village Panchayats, no specific powers have been assigned to them. Thus the Gram Sabhas have not attained their due importance in most of the states.

The provisions regarding the formation of intermediate level of Panchayats have been made mandatory even for small states like Kerala. Only the states having population not exceeding twenty lakhs are excluded from these provisions. In fact, in small states like Kerala there is no need for the formation of intermediate level Panchayats. At least the states should have been given freedom in this regard.

Another drawback of the Constitutional Amendment is in respect of the exclusion of urban areas from the District Panchayats. While there are three levels of Panchayats for every rural area, *viz.* village, intermediate and district, a single tier system exists for urban area. The urban areas should have been included in the district set up and the Municipalities should have been made a lower level local government. Because of this discrepancy, the concept of district government at the district level is not materialized. The Constitutional Amendments permit the state legislatures to make MPs and MLAs as members in the Local Self-Government Institutions. This is against the spirit of decentralisation. The local governments are the bodies responsible for local development whereas the MPs and MLAs are the members of legislative bodies and in a way they are the part of the Central and State administration respectively. Their inclusion in the local bodies will permit them to interfere in the local administration and such interference is not at all advisable in the interests of decentralisation. The Constitutional Amendments provide for the dissolution of local governments at the discretion of the state governments. This is against the spirit of autonomy, especially since Article 356 regarding the dissolution of state governments by the Centre is frequently misused. Though the Constitution provides for the reservation of seats and offices of chairpersons to the Scheduled Castes, Scheduled Tribes and women and for the rotation of these seats and offices, no specific principles have been laid down for following the rotation. This has led to many practical problems and ambiguity. The Constitutional Amendments are silent on the administrative powers of the local self-government institutions over the staff under them. The provisions relating to planning are quite vague. The powers of the District Planning Committee are limited to the integration of the Plans prepared by the urban and rural local self-governments and its submission to the state government. There is no mention about the state government's role on the plan proposals of the District Planning Committees. The Constitutional Amendments should have brought out an effective and fool-proof system for the audit of accounts of the Local Self-Government Institutions (V.J. Thankappan 2000:7).

The Kerala leftists found fault with the conformity legislation of the State enacted by the UDF Government led by Congress(I). CPI(M) leader, V.J. Thankappan who worked as the Vice-Chairman of the Administrative Reforms Committee articulated the drawbacks of the Kerala Act, 1994, enacted by the previous Congress led government in the following manner:

> The Kerala Panchayat Raj Act enacted in 1994, though contains many progressive and democratic provisions, was not free from drawbacks. Section 159 thereof enabled the government to remove the President, Vice-President or any member of the Panchayat from his office on grounds such as misconduct in the discharge of his duties, abuse of powers and persistent default in the performance of duties. The persons thus removed from office could be disqualified from becoming a member again, for a period not exceeding five years. This provision was more drastic than the power of the President of India to dismiss an elected state government. The provision for dissolution of a Panchayat under Section 193 also was undemocratic, if not unconstitutional. Section 191 empowered the state government to cancel

> any resolution or decision or action of the Panchayat on any flimsy ground. This provision was intended to divert the powers of the Panchayats. Two main subjects which were concerned with the common man, *viz.* rural water supply and rural electrification, were left out from the functions assigned to the Panchayats and these functions were allowed to be attended to by the Kerala Water Authority and the State Electricity Board respectively. In respect of minor irrigation schemes, the function of village Panchayats was restricted in so far as they could take up schemes benefiting up to five hectares. In fact a small village tank will have the capacity to irrigate more than five hectares. The dual control over the staff by the Panchayat and the government was vaguely worded and there was scope for friction between the Panchayats and the Government staff transferred to them. The administrative control of the Panchayats over the staff was restrictive. The provisions relating to Gram Sabhas were not exhaustive and they had not been given any worthwhile powers. The Gram Sabha provisions should have been made so clear that it could function as a link between the people and their administrators, vested with powers required therefor (*ibid.* : 11).

It was to rectify the above noted drawbacks that the LDF government appointed the Committee on Decentralisation of powers under the Chairmanship of S.B. Sen. The committee laid down its basic principles within a period of three weeks. The guiding principles of the Sen Committee are the following:

1. *Autonomy*: The LSGIs are to be autonomous, functionally, financially and administratively. The different tiers of LSGIs should be seen as complementary units rather than hierarchically organised.

2. *Subsidiarity*: It meant that what can be done best at a particular level should be done at that level and not at higher levels. All that can be optimally done at the lowest level should be reserved to that level. Only the residual should be passed on to the higher levels.

3. *Role clarity*: There should be clarity at conceptual and operational levels regarding the role of each tier in the development process and clear division of functions between the tiers.

4. *Complementarity*: The functions of different tiers should not be overlapping, but should be complementary to each other.

5. *Uniformity*: There should be uniformity of norms and criteria for pattern of assistance or selections of beneficiaries for all the programmes being implemented in a local area irrespective of the sponsoring agency.

6. *People's participation*: The functioning of the local self-government should be such that it facilitates maximum direct participation of people in the development process. The participation should be empowered and deliberative.

7. *Accountability*: The accountability of the elected representative is usually confined to the periodic electoral verdicts. Instead, there should be continuous social auditing of performance.

8. *Transparency*: People should have the right to information regarding every details of the administration.

The committee suggested comprehensive amendments to the existing Acts as per the guiding principles mentioned above.

As we noted earlier, on the basis of the recommendations of the Sen Committee, the government amended the Kerala Panchayati Raj Act, 1994 and the Kerala Municipal Act, 1994 at the end of 1999.

The salient features of the amended local bodies' Acts are given below:

Autonomy of the local bodies increased by reducing the state government's interference in the day-to-day functioning of local bodies. The state government cannot dissolve a local body arbitrarily. Before initiating the process of dissolution the government has to get opinion from an independent authority. The amendment enacted in 1999 took away the control of the State government and its functionaries over the LSGIs.

The amendments redefined the powers and functions of different tiers of local bodies by applying the principles of subsidarity, complementarity and role clarity. It has been decided that the relationship among the three tiers should not be on a hierarchical basis. At the same time there should be complementarity among the three tiers. The amendments provided more role clarity for each tier by classifying the powers and functions into a number of categories, *viz.* mandatory functions, regulatory functions, directive functions, agency functions, management functions, participatory functions, complementary functions and agency functions.

Provisions for ensuring transparency have been incorporated in the Act. As per the provisions all plan documents are public documents and citizen can have access to it. Details of public works are to be exhibited on Notice Boards. All information should be made available to the public if demanded and denial of access to information is a punishable offence. The most important provision as part of transparency is the requirement for the publication of citizens' charter with in six months of assuming office by the new Panchayat Committee. The citizens' charter should spell out clearly the services which it guarantees to the citizen. In addition to the transparency concept, measures have been introduced to control corruption. At the bottom level, social auditing by the Gram Sabha has been promoted as a measure against corruption. Another most important institution introduced to provide checks and balances is the Ombudsman consisting of seven members—a High Court Judge, two District Judges, two Secretaries to government and two public men selected in consultation with the leader of opposition to the State Legislative Assembly. The Ombudsmanic institution has been given enough powers to function as a watchdog against nepotism and corruption by the local body functionaries. This institution has been empowered to take corrective measures and impose punishment if warranted. (As we noted earlier the next UDF Government dissolved the seven members Ombudsman and replaced it with a single member).

The Sen Committee recommended the establishment of an Appellate Tribunal at the regional/district level to act as a grievance redressal mechanism, where individuals can appeal against the decisions of the local bodies while exercising their regulatory roles like issue of licence, grant of persuit, etc. The head of the Appellate Tribunal shall be an official in the rank of a District Judge.

It is expected that these two institutions—Ombudsman and Appellate Tribunal—would help the protection of the autonomy of the local bodies and restrict the undue interference of the bureaucracy in the day-to-day functioning of the local bodies as also ensure protection to the rights of citizen if the local bodies exercise their powers arbitrarily.

Administrative decentralisation and financial devolution have increased the importance of proper audit. In Kerala, the auditing of local funds has been entrusted with the Local Fund Audit Department, which is very much part of the State Government. Under the new situation of massive devolution of funds to local bodies by the State Government, it was felt that local fund auditing should be done by an independent Local Fund Audit Commission. The Sen Committee made recommendations for strengthening the Audit System. It recommended the introduction of Performance Audit.

Another very important institution recommended by the Sen Committee is the formation of a State Development Council. This is to be headed by the Chief Minister. All ministers shall be members of the council. Other members of the council shall be the leader of the Opposition, Vice-Chairman of the State Planning Board, the Chief Secretary, all the District Panchayat Presidents and representatives of other tiers of local governments.

The main amendments enacted in 1999 as per the Sen Committee recommendations can be summarized as follows:

1. The powers and functions of Gram Sabhas have been enlarged so as to empower the people to control the elected body. In Kerala unlike in other States, each constituency of the village Panchayat has a Gram Sabha.

2. The number of seats in the Gram Panchayat and Block Panchayats has been increased from the existing 8-15 range to 10-20 range so that the Gram Sabha can function effectively. The strength in the District Panchayat has been increased from 15-25 range to 15-30 range.

3. The number of Standing Committees is increased, from 1 to 3 in Gram Panchayats from 2 to 3 in Block Panchayats and from 4 to 5 in District Panchayats. Every elected member of the Panchayat

will become a member of any of the standing committees. This will enable all elected persons to become part of the administrative and decision-making machinery.

4. The members of the Parliament and Legislative Assembly are prohibited from becoming the members of the local governments.

5. All functions connected with the conduct of elections to the local bodies, including ward delimitation and reservation of seats, are entrusted with the State Election Commission.

6. District/Regional Tribunals are appointed as appellate authorities to dispose of the appeals on the orders/action of the LSGIs and these tribunals are drawn from the cadre of District Judges.

7. To detect corruption and to impose penalties on the guilty, an Ombudsmanic Institution was established.

8. If any member of the Local Self-Government Institution is found guilty of corruption, misappropriation of funds, loss of public money, etc., he is liable to forfeiture of his membership. He is also forbidden in contesting the next elections. The loss made would be realized from him.

9. The President/Chairperson is made the executive head of LSGIs.

10. The elected members are made liable to declare their assets within three months of their election.

11. Every employee of the LSGIs including the government employee is made responsible to attend to any duty assigned to him by the LSGIs.

12. The secretary and other employees are given more responsibilities with regard to the execution of the decisions of the elected body.

13. The senior government officers transferred to the LSGIs are made its *ex-officio* secretaries.

14. Plan preparation, publication of administration report and timely vetting of the budget are made mandatory duties of LSGIs.

15. The provisions relating to building tax, profession tax, advertisement tax, etc. are modified to enlarge the revenue base of the LSGIs.

16. In consideration of fast pace of urbanisation the building regulations are extended to the village Panchayat areas.

17. The provisions relating to solid waste management and public health in the Panchayat areas are strengthened.

18. The provisions relating to the "Right to Information" in respect of the affairs of the LSGIs are incorporated in the enactments.

19. The LSGIs are made liable to publish citizens' character indicating the services they will render to the public and the time limit taken therefor.

20. The schedules relating to mandatory and developmental functions are recast, re-defining the areas of each item therein and adding some new items.

Transfer of Development Departments and Staff

Immediately after assuming of power by the newly elected local bodies in September 1995, the State Government transferred a part of major development institutions and the staff managing them to the respective local bodies. The administration of *Krishi Bhavans,* Veterinary sub-centres/hospitals, *Anganavadis* and *Balawadis,* Primary Health Centres, Ayurvedic and Homoeo dispensaries and lower primary schools was transferred to Gram Panchayats. Block Panchayats were given the administration of care homes, old age homes, pre-metric hostels, community health centres and laboratory. District agriculture farms, district level animal husbandry institutes, fisheries schools, upper primary schools, high schools, training centres were transferred to District Panchayats. Beside the staff who were working in these institutions also got transferred to the respective local body institution. This has tremendously changed the structure and staff pattern in LSGIs.

The Structure, Powers and Functions of Gram Sabha

The powers and functions of the Village Assembly (*Gram Sabha*) have been enhanced. Even though the 73rd and 74th Amendment to the Constitution of India mandated the convening of Gram Sabha in all villages and ward committees in all urban areas, the right to decide the powers, functions, responsibilities and activities of these local body assemblies have been left to the respective State Governments. Based on this enactment at the Union level the government of the State of Kerala incorporated provisions in its Panchayati Raj Act and Municipalities Act, 1994. The structure and functions of Gram Sabhas are provided in Section 3 of Kerala Panchayati Raj Act 1994. They are:

1. Each Ward of a Gram Panchayat can be considered as a village for the formation of Gramsabhas.

2. Gram Sabha will consist of all electorates belonging to the territorial area of the Ward concerned.

3. Gram Sabhas must be convened minimum two times in a year. (The number of meetings have been increased from two to four by the Amendment in 1999).

4. The quorum of the meeting has been fixed as 50 persons. (This has been increased to 100 persons or ten per cent of the total voters, which ever is less).

5. The elected member representing the Ward/Constituency in the Gram Panchayat shall be the convener of the Gram Sabha concerned.

6. The Gram Panchayat has to place its annual reports before the Gram Sabha.

7. The recommendations and suggestions of Gram Sabha have to be given due consideration by all the tiers of the local government.

8. The functions of Gram Sabha are:

(a) To render help in preparing developmental schemes for the villages. To monitor and evaluate the implementation of development programmes.

(b) To nurture the sense of unity and harmony among the different groups of people.

(c) To mobilise voluntary work, to collect money or things for social development schemes.

(d) To involve in the implementation of developmental schemes pertaining to the village.

(e) To identify beneficiaries for the developmental programmes and schemes.

(f) Implementation of literacy programmes in the village.

(g) To discuss the reports of Gram Panchayat and development activities. To submit suggestions and recommendations about the development activities.

(h) Other functions as specified.

9. Resolutions shall be adopted on a majority basis.

10. The procedures for convening and conducting Gram Sabha shall be as specified.

The rules and regulations for the conduct of Gram Sabha are mainly four in number.

1. The Gram Sabha meetings shall be conducted between 8 a.m. and 6 p.m.

2. The date, time and venue of the Gram Sabha meetings shall be displayed in common places, Government offices, schools, villages and Panchayat offices.

3. The Secretary of the Gram Panchayat in consultation with the President shall prepare a programme schedule which shall include matters to be discussed in the Gram Sabha.

The amendments to the original enactments, adopted as per the recommendations of the Sen Committee report mandated the establishment of Ward Assemblies similar to Gram Sabhas in urban areas, except large Municipalities and Municipal Corporations. In tribal areas separate tribal assemblies are made mandatory. The Sen Committee wanted to promote participatory community structure like beneficiary committees and neighbourhood groups. Enabling provisions have been added in the local body Acts to encourage organising of such participatory structures at the bottom layer of the grassroots. The amendment enhanced the role of Gram Sabha as a mechanism for social audit. Review reports pertaining to Plan implementation and Panchayat administration are to be placed before the Gram Sabha. The responsibility of selection of beneficiaries for various schemes has been entrusted with the gram

Sabha. The role of the elected ward member in the selection of beneficiaries is limited to the fixation of criteria and the invitation of application form. As per the newly incorporated provisions in the Act it is the duty of the Gram Sabha to identify the eligible individuals and families and prepare the priority list.

4. The resolutions that are adopted on a majority basis in the Gram Sabha shall be informed to the concerned Panchayat within a week.

In this chapter we have summarized the political vision, various phases of the campaign and the administrative reforms initiated. It also briefly presented the various measures taken by the State Government to empower local bodies. With this background in mind we are proceeding to two village panchayats to make a detailed examination of the way in which the decentralised planning was carried out at the grassroots level.

3

DECENTRALISED PLANNING AND DEVELOPMENT IN ACTION AT THE LOCAL LEVEL

Two village Panchayats in Thiruvananthapuram district has been selected for field study. Among the two selected one Panchayat is controlled by the CPI(M) and the other by the Congress(I). One LDF Panchayat and one UDF Panchayat has been selected with a view to understand the extent to which a development culture beyond partisan interests emerged in Kerala as a result of the people's campaign for decentralized planning.

I

KUDAPPANAKUNNU–GRAM PANCHAYAT

Kudappanakunnu is a special grade Gram Panchayat in the suburb of the city corporation of Thiruvananthapuram. It is part of the Thiruvananthapuram Rural Block Panchayat and Thiruvananthapuram Taluk. Total area of the Panchayat is 7.69 sq.kms. In its Southern border, it is Thiruvananthapuram City Corporation; North Karakulam Panchayat; West Ulloor Panchayat (Recently Ulloor Panchayat was dissolved and the area was amalgamated into Thiruvananthapuram Corporation). This Panchayat is controlled by Congress(I). As per 1991 census, the total population of this Panchayat is 33,534. Among these, 17,008 are females and 16,506 are males. It is estimated that 1,949 are children below six years. Development Report of the Panchayat says that unemployment is a severe problem in this Panchayat. The

Panchayat Development Report further says that a chain of wet lands, which were used for rice cultivation was the predominant feature of this area some fifty years back. Any number of small streams and ponds were the hallmark of the Panchayat area at that time. The present situation is pitiable. Wet lands have been converted into dry land and rice cultivation has come down substantially. The hard reality today is that no cultivator is interested in rice cultivation due to obvious reasons. The generally felt feeling is that paddy cultivation is no longer feasible. Therefore, wet lands have shrunk into alarming proportions. The reclaimed wet lands have been sold out at attractive prices for the construction of dwelling units and commercial complexes. The near total distress situation in the area in rice cultivation should not be wrongly understood as development of cash crops and people have found out other profitable avenues in agricultural activities. The truth is that there is total stagnation in agricultural sector.

The Development Report prepared as part of the PCDP, says that this Panchayat was self-reliant in food production once. Apart from large stretches of paddy fields, coconut farms and banana farms were characteristic features of this area. Substantial portion of paddy fields were reclaimed. Other agricultural activities also have come down. Even though, this Panchayat is sharing boarder with the capital city, no industry worth the name could be found in any part of the Panchayat. At the same time, the number of unemployed is more than 23,000. On the whole the conditions of other sectors are also not satisfactory.

On the basis of the need identification in Gram Sabha and subsequent discussions in the Development seminar a shelf of projects were prepared for the total development of this Panchayat. As per the guidelines of the SPB these projects were prepared by the task forces constituted in the Panchayat. From out of this shelf of projects, the Panchayat picked up projects on a priority basis according to the allocation earmarked for it. SPB had asked all the Panchayats to earmark 40 to 50 per cent for productive sectors (Agriculture, Animal Husbandry, Fisheries, Small Industries), 30 to 40 per cent for social sectors (Health, Education, Water Supply, Sanitation, etc.) and 10 to 30 per cent for infrastructure (Roads etc.).

However, as revealed by Table 3.1 in the first year of PCDP, only 27.16 per cent was actually spent in productive sector. It came down to 11.99 per cent in second year and 8.74 per cent in the third year. In the fourth year the amount spent in the productive sector is a megre 1.72 per cent only. In the year 1997-98, 28.30 percentage of the total fund was utilized for implementing projects in the social sector. It was increased to 42.79 in the year 1998-99. There was a substantial increase (57.79 per cent) in the third year of PCDP. The fourth year witnessed a marginal decrease in social sector spending (43.35 per cent). In the inaugural year of PCDP, infrastructure projects were limited to 15.53 per cent. It increased to 31.39 in the second year. It became 33.5 per cent in the third year. The fourth year witnessed substantial increase (43.38 per cent) in the quantum of amount spent on infrastructure projects. Projects implemented in the SC/ST sector showed a down ward trend from 29.02 per cent in the first year to 11.54 per cent in the fourth year. In 1999-2000 no amount was spent on SC/ST sector. The trend is continued decrease in spending on productive and SC/ST development sectors. This is as a result of more spending on social sector and infrastructure development.

Table 3.1 : Expenditure on Projects (in Percentage)—Sectorwise

	Years			
Sector	**1997-98**	**1998-99**	**1999-2000**	**2000-01**
Productive	27.16	11.99	8.74	1.72
Social	28.30	42.79	57.79	43.35
Infrastructure	15.53	31.39	33.5	43.38
SC/ST	29.02	13.75	Nil	11.54
Total	100.00	100.00	100.00	100.00

Source : Kudappanakunnu Panchayat Documents on PCDP.

The sector-wise details of projects implemented are given in Table 3.2. In the productive sector Agriculture received 12.79 per cent in the first year. In the same year amount spent on Animal Husbandry projects was 14.37 per cent. Animal Husbandry received comparatively good attention in the second year also. It should be noted that Industry did not receive proper attention during the period under study During 1997-98 and 2000-01 no amount was spent for industrial development. It should also be noted that no project was implemented exclusively for women development.

Table 3.2 : Expenditure on Projects (in Percentage)

Sector	1997-98	1998-99	1999-2000	2000-01
Agriculture	12.79	1.02	4.65	1.51
Animal Husbandry	14.37	10.41	1.69	0.21
Industry	Nil	0.56	2.4	Nil
Infrastructure	14.14	21.07	24.46	39.48
Energy	1.39	10.39	9.04	3.9
Education	11.29	21.17	2	5.84
Health	Nil	10.49	4.45	1.13
Drinking water	Nil	Nil	Nil	1.56
Housing	Nil	11.13	51.34	34.82
Social welfare	17.01	Nil	Nil	Nil
Women Development	Nil	Nil	Nil	Nil
SC/ST	29.02	13.75	Nil	11.54
TOTAL	100.00	100.00	100.00	100.00

Source : Kudappanankkunnu Panchayat Office Document on PCDP.

The nature and quality of the projects implemented are also important. As we have already noted the amount spent for agriculture during 1997-98 was 12.79 per cent. Five projects were implemented in this sector and all these five were subsidy based and meant for benefits to individuals. Not even a single project was there for any kind of commercialisation of agriculture. The story is not different in successive years.

The development report of the Panchayat had identified the problems in the agriculture sector and made a few suggestions to solve these problems. The project implemented in the agriculture sector is required to be evaluated against the backdrop of the need identification and situation analysis done at the beginning of PCDP.

The greatest problem identified in the development report was the lack of interest for rice cultivation. Substantial area of paddy lands were reclaimed and were used for commercial purposes. This had affected the number of small rivers and streams that were previously part of the paddy field chain. The disappearance of water streams had led to scarcity of drinking water. Therefore, according to the report, the need of the hour was reclamation of paddy lands and water sources linked to paddy fields. Even though paddy development projects were implemented, the net outcome was not encouraging. The development report emphasized the need for the promotion of other agricultural sectors. Among these were commercial horticulture and mushroom farming. Also the Development report had identified certain agro-based industries such as coconut-processing unit, coconut fibre focused industries, soft drinks based on coconut water, etc. However, no such projects were undertaken.

Table 3.3 provided the details of the projects implemented in agricultural sector in the year 1997-98. Rupees 72,370 (6.2 per cent)

Table 3.3 : Expenditure on projects in Productive Sector (1997-98)

Sl.No.	Project name	Amount spent (Rs.)	%	Achievements
1.	Integrated Paddy cultivation	72,370	6.2	Paddy cultivation extended upto 9.64 Hectres
2.	Vegetable cultivation	45,767	3.92	223 kitchen gardens came into being
3(a)	Integrated Coconut Development	2,90,080	24.83	Fertilizer kits distributed among 500 cultivators
(b)	Banana cultivation	1,28,136	10.97	Assistance extended to 185 cultivators
(c)	Tuber crops	13,647	1.67	Encouraged 91 cultivators
4.	Egger Nursery	7,000	0.6	Provided chikens for distribution in the Panchayat
5.	Backward poultry farm	1,14,075	9.78	351 families were supplied with 10 chickens each
6.	Goat farming	90,740	7.77	88 families benefited
7.	Broiler chicken farm	45,000	3.85	provided employment for 15 unemployed
8.	Rabbies control	19,680	1.68	700 domestic dogs vaccinated
9.	Fish farming	1,24,925	10.7	Fresh water ponds in the Panchayats were cleaned and made available for fresh water fish farming
10	Poultary Farm	1,80,480	15.45	Extended help to 525 poor families to increase their income
11.	Furniture for veterinary hospital	36,230	3.10	Amenities improved
	TOTAL	11,68,130	100	

Source : Kudappanakunnu Panchayat Office Document on PCDP.

had been spent for reclamation of paddy land. As a result paddy cultivation extended upto 9.64 hectors.

Apart from paddy cultivation development, Kudappanakunnu paid due attention to vegetable (Rs.45,767) cultivation, Banana cultivation (Rs.12,8136) and coconut development (Rs.2,90,080). From the above it can be noted that major portion of the fund went for integrated coconut development (24.83 per cent). 500 coconut cultivators received one fertilizer kit each. Likewise 185 banana cultivators received financial assistance for banana cultivation. Similarly, 223 kitchen gardens were developed for improving the supply of vegetables to the local market.Other important projects implemented in the productive sector during 1997-98 are in the animal husbandry sector. An egger nursery was established by spending Rs.7,000. 351 families in the Panchayats have been provided with 10 chickens each for establishing backyard poultry farm. 88 families were given help in establishing goat farm by spending Rs.90,740. By spending Rs.40,000, fifteen unemployed youth were helped to start Broiler Chicken farm. Fresh water ponds in the Panchayats were cleaned and made available for fresh water fish farming. For this the expenditure incurred was Rs.1,24,925. The projects extended help to 525 poor families to increase their income by starting poultry farm. The amount spent for this purpose was Rs. 1,80,480.700 domestic dogs were vaccinated by spending Rs.19,680. The veterinary hospital in the Panchayat received Rs.36,230 for the purchase of furniture.

In the animal husbandry sector, in addition to subsidy-based projects for the development of individuals, households, dissemination of new knowledge and technologies was suggested. The emphasis was on the supply of milch animals and birds to individual farmers. This was done without designing adequate measures to see that the beneficiaries who received it did not sell out the animals and birds supplied. In the industry sector two projects undertaken failed to achieve its objectives.

During 1997-98 the infrastructure sector received Rs.6,11,070 (See Table 3.4). The achievement in this sector during the said period is reported as repair works in the existing roads in the Panchayats.

Table 3.4 : Expenditure on Projects in Infrastructure Sector (1997-98)

Sl. No.	Name of Project	Amount spent (in Rs.)	%	Achievements
1.	Roads-Darsan Nagar road	87,825	14.37	Existing roads were repaired
2.	Maruppancode road	2,59,925	42.54	,,
3.	Muttada NSS Mazhuvan-cherry	75,000	12.27	Roads repaired
4.	NCC road	60,487	9.9	,,
5.	Thumbikonam surplus land road	75,000	12.27	,,
6.	NCC Nagar road	50,000	8.18	,,
7.	Trainee Allowance (Engineer)	2,833	0.46	Strengthened the engineering wing of the Panchayat
	TOTAL	6,11,070	100	

Source : Kudappanankunnu Panchayat Office Document on PCDP

In the social sector during 1997-98 nine projects were implemented by spending Rs.13,46,992 (See Table 3.5). Of this Rs.2,44,000 had been spent for the construction of latrines for 160 poor families. By spending Rs.2,91,067 basic amenities in the three *anganvadis* were improved. Rs.1,23,750 had been spent for the construction of houses for five poor families. Other important projects implemented during this period in the social sector included purchase of books for rural libraries and purchase of furniture for the schools in the Panchayat. Rs.27,225 had been spent for the purchase of CFL lamps. Eight projects were implemented during the period for SC/ST development by spending Rs.11,14,404 (See Table 3.6). Substantial portion of the amount (Rs. 4,82,154) had been spent for extending drinking water pipe lines to scheduled caste colonies. By implementing this project drinking water problem in SC colonies had been solved. Second most important project for the SC development was the concreting of SC colony roads by spending Rs.2,55,891. The physical achievement reported is that the colony roads were made motorable.

Table 3.5 : Expenditure on Projects in Social Sector (1997-98)

Sl. No.	Name of project	Amount spent (in Rs)	%	Achievement
1.	Smokeless Choolah	32,600	2.42	Supplied to 400 families
2. (a)	Furniture for schools PSNMBHS Peroor-kada	1,50,645	11.18	Basic amenities improved in schools
(b)	UPS Kudappanakunnu	2,09,800	15.58	,,
(c)	UPS Kusavarkal	65,200	4.84	,,
3.	Grants for Rural Libraries	60,000	4.45	Books of quality distributed to rural libraries in the Panchayat
4.	Latrine for poor families	2,44,000	18.11	Constructed latrines for 160 families
5.	Medical camp	72,705	5.4	Organised six medical camps
6.	Anganvadi community hall	2,91,067	21.61	Improved basic amenities in three anganvadis
7.	Housing for poor families	1,23,750	9.18	Financial assistance for the construction of five houses
8.	Distribution of CFL	27,225	2.02	Energy conservation
9.	Building for 38 Anganwadi	70,000	5.2	Completed first phase
	TOTAL	13,46,992	100	

Source : Kudappanakunnu Panchayat Office Document on PCDP.

Another major project is the construction of six tube wells in SC colonies by spending Rs.1,94,215. By spending Rs.19,000, latrines were constructed for 52 families. Other important projects implemented are supply of uniform to 500 school children (Rs.82,144) and renovation of *Balvadies* and *Anganvadies* in SC colonies. The Physical achievements are improvement of educational and entertainment facilities for SC children.

In Kudappanakunnu, more money had been spent on infrastructure. In 1997-98, it was 15.53 per cent. In 2000-01 total expenditure on infrastructure was 43.38 per cent. Substantial portion of this had been spent on road construction.

Table 3.6 : Expenditure on projects in the SC/ST Development Sector (1997-98)

Sl. No.	Project's name	Expenditure (in Rs)	%	Achievement
1.	Tube wells in SC colonies	1,94,215	17.43	Six tube wells constructed
2.	Uniform distribution for SC School Children	82,144	7.37	500 School children benefited
3.	Latrines	19,000	1.70	Latrines for 52 families
4.	Concreting of SC Colony roads	2,55,891	22.96	Roads were made motorable
5.	Extension of Drinking water pipe line to SC colonies	4,82,154	43.27	Drinking water problems in colonies solved
6.	Maintenance and repair work of balawadi at SC colony	45,000	4.04	SC Children's educational and entertainment facilities improved
7.	Renovation of crèche at SC colony	20,000	1.79	Health care facility
8.	Renovation of Anganwadi at Harvipuram SC colony	16,000	1.44	Basic amenities improved
	TOTAL	11,14,404	100	

Source : Kudappanakunnu Panchayat Office Document on PCDP.

However Table 3.1 reveals that highest spending had been on social sector. In 1999-2000 social sector spending reached 57.79 per cent. In 1998-99 21.17 per cent was spent on education. In 1999-2000 and 2000-01, 51.34 per cent and 34.82 per cent were spent on housing respectively. In 1997-98 other social sector activities received a support of 17.01 per cent.

Eleven projects were implemented in productive sector during 1998-99 (See Table 3.7). The major project of this period was the financial assistance provided to 63 families for the purchase of milch cows. Total amount spent for this project was Rs.6,19,996. The second important project implemented during the period was in the agriculture sector for the expansion of paddy cultivation. By spending Rs.26,975, paddy cultivation extended to another 4.32

hectares. Third important project got implemented in animal husbandry sector. 123 families were given 5 chickens each by spending Rs.24,600. The achievement expected was increase in egg production through the development of backyard poultry farm.

Table 3.7 : Expenditure on Projects Implemented in Productive Sector (1998-99)

Sl. No.	Project's Name	Expenditure (31.3.99) (in Rs)	%	Achievements
1.	Expansion of paddy cultivation	26,975	3.5	Extended paddy cultivation 4.32 to hectare
2.	Inter crops	16,500	2.14	Distributed seeds to 165 small scale farmers
3.	Vegetable cultivation gardens	3,250	0.42	325 kitchen are established.
4.	Mushroom cultivation	1,620	0.21	Encouragement for 6 cultivators
5.	Basic Amenities in Krishi Bhavan	10,000	1.26	Furniture were purchased for Krishi Bhavan
6.	Honouring best cultivators	7,500	0.97	Encouragement is given to ten cultivators
7.	Animal Husbaddry Backyard poultry farm	24,600	3.19	5 chickens are given to 123 families. Egg production increased
8.	Rabies control	16,950	2.2	Vaccination were given to 230 domestic dogs
9.	Improvement of amenities in veterinary hospitals	8,424	1.09	One microscope each is given to two veterinary hospitals
10.	Milch cow scheme	6,19,996	80.32	Financial aid is given to 63 farmers for purchase of milch cows
11.	Manufacturing unit for electronic chokes	36,000	4.66	Working capital for it deposited in the District cooperative bank
	TOTAL	25,06,800	100	

Source : Kudappanakunnu Panchayat Office Document on PCDP.

In 1998-99 Rs.16,950 had been spent for Rabies control. 230 domestic dogs were vaccinated. Other important projects of the said period are vegetable cultivation, mushroom cultivation, improvement of basic amenities in agricultural office and veterinary hospitals. Also an attempt had been made for the establishment of an electronic choke manufacturing unit in the Panchayat.

In the matter of projects for SC development, in 1997-98, the spending was 29.02 per cent, in 1998-99 it was 13.75 per cent and 11.54 per cent in 2000-01. Major portion of the fund earmarked for SC Development also spent on social and infrastructure sectors. On the whole virtually no investment in productive sector could be noticed in Kudappanakunnu.

The projects implemented in social sector during 1998-99 were mainly for development of education. For improving the educational standards of LP school students coming from poor families, special tuitions were arranged by spending Rs.26,768. 200 poor school children benefited out of this project. By spending Rs.1,13,044 nutritional foods were supplied to LP school students. 10,000 students coming from poor families got the benefit of this project. By spending Rs.1,92,004 mid-day meal scheme was implemented in LP schools. From this project also 10,000 poor students benefited.

Anemia control, chlorination and mosquito control were the notable projects implemented in the Panchayat during 1998-99. Anemia control project brought in benefits for women and children. By spending Rs.16,614 drinking water wells numbering 2228 were chlorinated. Mosquito control measures like sprinkling oil in pools and unhygienic surroundings around 10,000 dwelling units were undertaken.

Rs.10,300 had been spent for the improvement of facilities in the public health centre. Similarly Rs.20,000 had been spent for the construction of latrine in the family welfare centre in the Panchayat. By spending Rs.16,484 two public taps were provided for the benefit of a few families in a BPL colony. 1000 women and children were provided with nutritional food through 31 *Anganvadis* by spending Rs.1,74,634. 140 families in the Panchayat were given financial assistance for the construction of latrines. The amount spent for this project was Rs.3,50,000. Fifty-three families received assistance for tile roofing of their houses. For the implementation of this project Rs.5,30,000 had been spent. Similarly 130 families

Table 3.8 : Expenditure on Projects Implemented in Social Sector (1998-99)

Sl. No.	Name of project	Total Expenditure	%	Achievements
1.	For improving the educational standard of LPS Students	26,768	1.54	Improved their standard by giving special tuition to 200 students
2.	Nutritional food distribution to LPS Students	1,13,044	6.52	Provided nutritional food for 10,000 students
3.	Mid-day meal for LPS students	1,92,004	3.75	10,000 school children benefited
4.	Scheme for taking over of pre-primary school	12,200	0.70	Panchayat has taken over of the pre-primary school of Kudappanakunnu LPS
5.	Anemia control	17,950	1.04	Women and children were benefited.
6.	Chlorination	16,614	0.09	2228 drinking water wells were chlorinated
7.	Mosquito control	53,787	3.10	Sprinkled oil in pools and unhygienic surroundings around 10,000 dwelling units.
8.	Improvement of primary facilities in PHC	10,300	0.59	Primary health centre benefited
9.	Latrine construction in Kusavarkkal family welfare centre	20,000	1.15	Improved the primary facilities
10.	Public Tap	16,484	0.95	2 taps were installed to solve drinking water problem
11.	Nutritional food for Anganvadi students and mothers	1,74,634	10.06	1000 women and children were provided nutritional food through 31 Anganwadis.
12.	Latrine construction	3,50,000	2.02	140 families were given financial assistance
13.	Furniture for Ayurvedic dispensary	15,200	0.88	Improved the basic facilities
14.	Housing Roof Tiles	5,30,000	30.55	53 houses tiled
15.	Separation of dwelling units in Laksham Veedu Housing colony	60,000	3.46	10 houses
16.	Thatching of houses	65,000	3.75	Financial assistance for thatching of 130 houses
17.	Projects expenditure	61,000	3.52	Expenditure for the implementation of the project
	TOTAL	17,34,985	100	

Source: Kudappanakunnu Panchayat Documents on PCDP.

received a total assistance of Rs.65,000 for thatching of their houses. Rs.60,000 had been spent for renovating and separating of the twin dwelling units in Laksham Veedu housing colony. The Ayurvedic dispensary of the Panchayat was supplied with new furniture by spending Rs.15,200.

The physical achievements reported from the road projects are the following: (1) side wall construction and mud filling, (2) concreting of roads, (3) re-tarring of roads, (4) construction of waste water canal, (5) construction of culverts and (6) metalling and tarring of new roads.

During 1998-99, on the whole 31 projects were implemented in the infrastructure sector. Of these, two projects were implemented in the power sector. Rs.6,45,200 had been spent for extension of electric lines for providing street light. Another 23,275 had been spent for the purchase of tube lights, bulbs choke, etc. The remaining 29 projects were implemented for road development in the Panchayat.

Table 3.9 : Expenditure on Projects implemented in Infrastructure Sector 1998-99

Sl. No.	Name of the Project	Expenditure (in Rs)	%	Achievements
1.	Energy Extension of electric lines for providing street light	6,45,200	31.88	Purchased tubes, chokes etc. and bulbs, extended electric line to new areas
2.	For purchasing electric goods	23,275	1.15	Tube,bulb,choke etc. are purchased
3.	Transport Kinavoor road (reconstruction)	23,000	1.13	230 m. side wall constructed and mud filling
4.	Mazhvancheri-Panayara road	10,000	.49	110m. side wall and mud filling
5.	Kunchuveedu lane road(re-construction)	10,000	.49	66 m Concrete road
6.	Nalanchira Parakodu lane wastewater canal construction	79,000	3.90	190 m waste water canal constructed
7.	Nalanchira-Anchumukku vayal re-tarring	50,000	2.47	500 m road was re-tarred
8.	Nalanchira Velanvila Ambanadu road reconnstruction	30,000	1.48	148 m side wall constructed
9.	Anchumukku vayal-Panayappalli road construction	53,000	2.62	224 m side wall and mudfilling
10.	Perubalaman road metalling tarring	20,000	.99	133 m road tarred

(Contd.)

Table 3.9 : (Contd.)

11.	Udiyanoor madathil Nada waste	32,000	1.58	110 m side wall water canal renovation constructed
12.	Ambanadu Malamel nada road	67,000	3.31	143 m side wall and mud reconstruction filling
13.	Pathirapalli panavila road	70,000	3.46	271 m road concrete, 28 m sidewall constructed
14.	Irripokuzhy - oarachani road	66,422	3.28	200 m side wall constructed
15.	Irripokuzhy-culvert	11,000	.54	Culvert constructed
16.	Nalumukku Idavazhi concrete	58,000	2.87	Constructed 120 m road
17.	Iruppukuzhi-pattukunnu road'swater canal construction	71,000	3.51	107.5 m canal constructed
18.	Mathilmukku Idavazhi concreted	18,000	.89	140 m road is concreted
19.	Yamuna colony Kunchila moodu road reconstruction	51,000	2.52	120 m side wall constructed
20.	CLHS road tarring	33,000	1.63	380 m road tarred
21.	Mulayarathala park road's reconstruction	1,47,000	7.26	180m side wall and mud filling
22.	Kanivilkathunaa road reconstruction	63,423	3.13	Side wall construction and mud filling
23.	Elluvila lane concrete	49,000	2.42	105 m road concreted
24.	Thekkemannamkonam Idavazhi concreted	49,000	2.42	90 m road concreted
25.	Sreenagar to Uliyanadu Pond road metalling and tarring	20,000	.99	160 m road's metalling and tarring started
26.	Kurunthotti Vilakam road concreting	41,160	2.03	73 m road concreted
27.	NCC Panavoor Thratta Vellamkolli road metalling and tarring	78,000	3.85	867 m road metalled and tarred
28.	SBT Prabhath lane concrete	40,000	1.98	130m road concreted
29.	Mannadi lane culvert	10,000	.49	1.5 × 1.5 side culvert constructed
30.	Panchayat office maintenance	26,608	1.31	Completed
31.	Oottukuzhi-Nedumbram Journalist colony road	78,376	3.87	152 m road concreted. And side wall constructed.
	TOTAL	20,23,464	100	

Source : Kudappanakunnu Panchayat Documents on PCDP.

During 1998-99 (Table 3.10) twelve projects were implemented for scheduled caste development. All the projects in this sector during the period targeted individual SC families in the Panchayat. Six SC families received financial assistance for the purchase of milch cows. The total amount spent for this project was Rs.57,000. Twelve SC families were given financial assistance (Rs.47,988) for the purchase of goats. Rs.3,70,000 had been spent for tiling of SC houses. Thirty-seven families benefited from this project. Rs. 16,000 had been spent for the construction of drinking water wells for the benefit of four families. By spending Rs.65,000, latrines

Table 3.10 : Expenditure on Projects Completed in the SC/ST Development Sector (1998-99)

Sl. No.	Name of Project	Expenditure (in Rs)	%	Achievements
1.	Milch cow	57,000	6.44	Financial assistance to 6 SC families for the purchase of milch cow
2.	Goat rearing	47,988	5.42	12 families got its benefit
3.	Tiling of houses	3,70,000	41.81	37 families enjoyed the benefit
4.	Drinking water wells	16,000	1.81	Wells for 4 families
5.	Latrine construction	65,000	7.35	26 families were beneficiaries
6.	Electrification of houses	22,350	2.52	40 families benefited
7.	Re-modelling Laksham veedu	67,500	7.63	10 houses were re-modelled and separated each other
8.	Construction of side wall and steps in Harveepuram colony	45,000	5.08	75 m road concreted
9.	Harveepuram children's park	45,041	5.09	Maintenance of children's park
10.	Harveepuram 1st lane road's re-construction	1,19,943	13.55	Re-constructed the road
11.	Puthuval Idavazhi Lane	12,000	1.36	Concrete work started
12.	Irappukuzhiputhuval waste water canal construction	17,000	1.92	Work in progress
	TOTAL	8,84,822	100	

Source : Kudappanakunnu Panchayat Documents on PCDP.

had been constructed for 26 families. For electrification of SC houses Rs.22,350 had been spent. Forty families benefited from this project. Rs. 67,000 had been spent for remodeling of Laksham veedu houses. 10 houses were separated from each other and re-modelled.

The remaining five projects were implemented for infrastructure development in SC colonies. For instance, by spending Rs.45,000, 75 metres road, side wall and steps in a SC colony were constructed. Concrete work in lanes and construction of waste water canal are other important infrastructure projects in the SC colonies.

Apart from this Rs. 45,000 had been spent for carrying out of maintenance work in the children's park in one of the SC colonies in the Panchayat.

Table 3.11 provides the details of the projects approved in the year 1998-99 and whose implementation spilled over into the next year.

Table 3.11 : Projects, which are approved in the year 1998-99 and need continuation (11) for completion

Sl.No	Project's Name	Expenditure
1	Integrated coconut cultivation	3,09,400
2	Labour contract co-operative society	1,00,000
3	Writing chalk production unit	2,00,000
4	Kuttattuvila ida roads (concrete)	1,00,000
5	Sree Chitra line road (taring)	85,000
6	Pullippara-Manjanpara road (mettaling and taring)	80,000
7	Kunnaravila Puthuchi road metalling	1,00,000
8	Jayaprakash line pullukulam surplus road mettaling and taring	1,00,000
9	Kuzhivila colony second line (second phase)	20,000
10	Construction of 38th Anganwadi	87,000
11	Irrappukuzhi-Patukunnu road	8,000
12	Harveepuram Anganvadi building	16,000
13	Reconstruction of Anchumukku Chuzhambala road	28,000

Source : Kudappanakunnu Panchayat Documents on PCDP.

Table 3.12 lists the projects implemented in productive sector in the year 1999-2000. On the whole eight projects were implemented. These projects are paddy development (Rs.17,823), coconut development (Rs.32,160), construction of Krishi Bhavan office (Rs.1,00,000), Coconut Pest control (Rs.1,39,523), Milch cow (Rs.83,124), Kamadhenu Insurance (Rs.6,867), Veterinary Hospital construction (Rs.50,000) and the Electronic choke manufacturing unit (Rs.2,00,000). On the whole Rs.7,29,497 had been spent for the implementation of various projects in the productive sector in 1999-2000.

Table 3.12 : Expenditure on Project Implemented in Productive Sector (1999-2000)

Sl. No.	Name of project	Expenditure (in Rs.)	%	Achievements
1.	Paddy Development	17,823	2.44	NA
2.	Coconut Development	1,32,160	18.12	NA
3.	Krishi Bhavan (construction)	1,00,000	13.71	NA
4.	Coconut pest control	1,39,523	19.12	NA
5.	Milch cow	83,124	11.39	NA
6	Kamadhenu Insurance	6,867	.94	NA
7	Vetenary hospital (Construction)	50,000	6.85	NA
8	Manufacturing unit	2,00,000	27.42	NA
	TOTAL	7,29,497	100	

Source : Kudappanakunnu Panchayat Documents on PCDP.

Table 3.13 provides the details of projects implemented in social sector during 1999-2000. Rs.48,76,834 had been spent for the implementation of fourteen projects in the sector. Noon meal scheme (Rs.56,000), nutritional food for school children (Rs.59,147) and nutritional food for *anganvadi* children (Rs.1,42,220) were the projects implemented for child development. A major portion of the amount spent during the year went for three housing projects (Rs.42,97,500). Rs.1,00,000 had been spent for the construction of drinking water wells. Purchase of library books, construction of compound wall for the library, repair of roof of the library building, electricity and water connection in the primary health centre and mosquito control projects are the other important projects implemented in social sector during 1999-2000.

Table 3.13 : Expenditure on Projects implemented in Social Sector 1999-2000

Sl. No.	Name of project	Expenditure (in Rs.)	%	Achievements
1.	Noon meal scheme	56,000	1.15	NA
2.	Nutritional food for school children	59,147	1.22	NA
3.	Library books	10,000	.21	NA
4.	Library-compound wall construction	23,000	.47	NA
5.	Library-roof repair	19,000	.39	NA
6.	Mosquito control	86,825	1.79	NA
7.	Primary health centre electricity and water connection	9,840	.20	NA
8.	Drinking water wells	1,00,000	2.07	NA
9.	Nutritional food for Anganwadi children	1,42,220	2.94	NA
10.	Anemia control	3,302	.07	NA
11.	Latrines	30,000	.62	NA
12.	Housing maintenance work	5,60,000	11.57	NA
13.	House-thatching	97,500	2.01	NA
14.	Housing-thanal scheme	36,40,000	75.25	NA
	TOTAL	48,36,834	100	

Source : Kudappanakunnu Panchayat Documents on PCDP.

In the infrastructure sector during 1999-2000, thirty-three projects were implemented by spending Rs.28,04,145. Among these four projects were in power sector. Rs.4,07,482 had been spent for CFL street lights. Another 1,40,000 rupees had been spent for ordinary street lights. Rs. 79,500 had been spent for house electrification. Rs. 1,30,000 had been spent for purchase of chokes for street lights.

Another 21 projects were implemented for road development. Road projects include construction of new roads, extension of existing roads, construction of side wall to the roads and undertaking repair works in existing roads. Total amount spent on road development is Rs. 7,75,648. Two waste water canals had been constructed by spending Rs.36,457. For providing basic amenities in a market in the Panchayat, Rs.65,000 had been spent. Rs.9,60,000 had been spent for the extension of pipe lines. The most important project during the period had been the allotment of 3 cents of land for the land less in the Panchayat by spending Rs. 9,60,000.

Table 3.14 : Expenditure on Projects implemented in Infrastructure Sector in 1999-2000

Sl. No.	Name of project	Expenditure (in Rs.)	%	Achievements
1.	CFL Street lights	4,07,482	14.53	NA
2.	Street lights	1,40,000	4.99	NA
3.	House electrification	79,500	2.83	NA
4.	Choke for street lights	1,30,000	4.63	NA
5.	Roads P.V.Thampi-Laksham veedu road	70,937	2.53	NA
6.	Kurunthotivilakam concrete road	21,258	.76	NA
7.	Siva Lane repair	47,674	1.70	NA
8.	Sevakendram road repair	50,429	1.79	NA
9.	Kytharatala Journalist road	45,799	1.63	NA
10.	Kunnumpuram Lane concrete	25,783	.92	NA
11.	Durgalane road re-tarring	62,236	2.22	NA
12.	Darsan nagar 2nd street	71,597	2.55	NA
13.	Pullumkulam colony road concrete	47,343	1.69	NA
14.	Marippancode side wall construction	70,165	2.50	NA
15.	Mangalathu lane concrete	33,584	1.19	NA
16.	Ootukuzhi waste sater canal	10,198	.36	NA
17.	Oonnampara Darsan nagar road	67,052	2.39	NA
18.	Nalanchira market	65,000	2.32	NA
19.	Harveepuram park	10,500	.37	NA
20.	Plan implementation	10,000	.35	NA
21.	Furniture for educational institutions	78,553	2.80	NA
22.	3 cents of land for landless	9,60,000	34.23	NA
23.	Harveepuram Kunnumpuram pipe lane extension	1,11,005	3.96	NA
24.	Vedanvila Ambanattu road	17,376	.62	NA
25.	Manamel Kaleelvila road	26,259	.94	NA
26.	Kuzhivila colony waste water canal	26,259	.94	NA
27.	Koottatuvila Edavazhi lane concrete	26,090	.93	NA
28.	Santi lane tarring	11,342	.40	NA
29.	Cherukala Lane concrete	5,160	.19	NA
30.	Nalanchira Kuzhakattu road repair	20,000	.71	NA
31.	Christian Medical Centre road tarring	23,896	.85	NA
32.	Valavumugal lane concrete	6,368	.23	NA
33.	Irapakuzhy Puthuval road	25,000	.89	NA
	TOTAL	28,04,145	100	

Source : Kudappanakunnu Panchayat Documents on PCDP.

During 2000-01 nine projects had been implemented in the productive sector by spending Rs.88,036 (Table 3.15). As is the case in previous years, the projects implemented in this sector were individual oriented. The physical achievements claimed by the Panchayat include the following: Self-reliance in vegetable supply, further improvement in paddy cultivation, pest control in coconut farms and improvement in irrigation facilities. This year also Rs.10,925 had been spent for Rabies control by vaccinating domestic dogs.

Table 3.15 : Expenditure on Projects Implemented in Productive Sector in 2000-01

Sl. No.	Name of project	Expenditure (in Rs.)	%	Achievements
1.	Paddy development	16,261	18.47	Priority for paddy develop ment
2.	Backyard vegetable Self-reliance in vegetable garden	1000	1.13	Supply
3.	Banana cultivation	9,350	10.62	Programme continues
4.	Tapioca	5,500	6.24	Programme continues
5.	Pest control (coconut)	7,000	7.95	Attempted to eradicate mandari pest from coconut trees
6.	Slaughtering of old coco nut trees	10,000	11.36	Old and sick trees felled
7.	Pump set	28,000	31.81	Irrigation facili ties improved
8.	Rabies control	10,925	12.41	Domestic dogs vaccinated
	TOTAL	88,036	100	

Source : Kudappanakunnu Panchayat Documents on PCDP.

The total expenditure incurred during 2000-01 for the implementation of social sector projects is Rs.23,03,648 (See table 3.16). Major projects implemented during the year are for housing development. A total of Rs.17,85,000 had been spent for housing scheme. Other projects are the repetition or continuation of the projects implemented in the previous years. The achievements of social projects reported during the year are the following:

(1) Noon meal for poor school children, (2) Improvement of basic facilities in *anganvadis,* (3) Purchase of books for rural libraries, (4) Purchase of TV sets for rural arts clubs, (5) Improvement of facilities for sports by constructing 5 swimming pools in the Panchayat, (6) Supply of medicine for Ayurvedic Hospital, (7) Supply of furniture for Homoeo hospital, and (8) Extension of pipe line.

Table 3.16 : Expenditure on Projects implemented in Social Sector in 2000-01

Sl. No.	Name of project	Expenditure (in Rs.)	%	Achievements
1.	Noon meal for school children	1,34,262	5.83	One time meal for poor school children
2.	Basic facilities in Anganwadi	68,814	2.99	Basic facilities improved
3.	Books for rural libraries	30,000	1.30	Rural libraries made people oriented
4.	TV for Arts club	18,850	.82	Cultural organizations were provided more facilities
5.	Swimming pool	30,000	1.30	Sports facilities improved
6.	Medicine for Ayurvedic hospital	40,000	1.74	Amenities provided
7.	Furniture for Homoeo hospital	18,000	.78	Amenities provided
8.	Cultural centre	17,670	.77	Encouraged cultural organisations
9.	Thanal Housing scheme	13,65,000	59.25	Housing facilities improved
10.	Thanal-Interest repayment	4,20,000	18.23	Repayment of interest
11.	Pipe line extension	80,000	3.47	Drinking water facilities improved
12.	Project implementation expenses	81,052	3.52	Project implementation expenses
	TOTAL	23,03,648	100	

Source : Kudappanakunnu Panchayat Documents on PCDP.

During 2000-01, three projects were implemented in the infrastructure sector by spending Rs.21,42,913. One project implemented for improving street lighting and another two projects were implemented for laying of new rural roads.

Table 3.17 : Expenditure on Projects Implemented in Infrastructure Sector in 2000-01

Sl. No.	Name of project	Expenditure (in Rs.)	%	Achievements
1.	Purchase of electrical goods	1,99,970	9.33	Street lighting improved
2.	Roads construction	17,62,931	82.27	Rural roads
3.	Roads construction	1,80,012	8.40	Rural roads
	TOTAL	21,42,913	100	

Source : Kudappanakunnu Panchayat Documents on PCDP.

Rs.1,78,717 had been spent in the SC development sector during 2000-01 (Table 3.18). The achievements of these projects include improvement of facilities in SC houses, purchase of land for the landless SCs, construction of rural roads through SC settlement areas and improvement of drinking water facilities in the SC colonies.

Table 3.18 : Expenditure on Projects implemented in SC/ST Sector in 2000-01

Sl. No.	Name of project	Expenditure (in Rs.)	%	Achievements
1.	House maintenance	10,000	5.59	Facilities improved in SC houses
2.	Land for landless	30,000	16.79	Provided land for land less SC
3.	Road	28,717	16.07	Rural roads through SC settlements materialized
4.	Drinking water wells	1,10,000	61.55	Drinking water facilities improved for SC families
	TOTAL	1,78,717	100	

Source : Kudappanakunnu Panchayat Documents on PCDP.

II

KARAKULAM GRAM PANCHAYAT

Karakulam Gram Panchayat consists of an area of 25.01 sq.kms. The boundaries of the Panchayat are Aruvikara Panchayat in the North-East, Vattiyurkavu Panchayat in the South-East, Kudappanakunnu Panchayat in the South-West, Ulloor and Sreekaryam Panchayats in the West and Nedumangad Municipality and Vembayam Panchayat in the North-West. It lies in the Nedumangad Block Panchayat in Thiruvananthapuram District. The Panchayat was created in 1953.

The population of the Panchayat is 40,503 (1991). 20,184 are males and 20,319 are females. The density of population is 1,617. There are 8,847 families. Average number of members in the families are 4.5—SC population is 3,905 : 1,856 males and 2,049 females.

Only 12,015 are employed. Some are partly employed 3,688 work in the agricultural sector. There are 17,991 unemployed women and 9,424 unemployed men. Many workers made a shift from the agricultural sector to the construction industry. Industries based on clay were popular once upon a time. But, when clay became unavailable, the industry faded away. For drinking water people depended on wells. During summer, some of the wells dried up. Public wells were not maintained well and so they became useless gradually. Paddy is the main crop. Other crops were coconut, arecanut, pepper, tapioca, banana, etc. Vegetables are also cultivated. One of the prestigious industries in Kerala is situated in the Panchayat—The Kerala State Electronics Development Corporation (Keltron). Other industries were in the areas of food processing, vessel manufacturing, hollow bricks, soap making, etc.

There are 10,100 houses in the Panchayat. 7,008 are electrified. Firewood is the main cooking fuel. Gas is also used for cooking purposes. There are many households where electricity is not available. Transportation facilities are being improved. Educationally, the Panchayat is better off. Majority is educated and almost all are literate.

Housing was a problem in the Panchayat at the beginning of PCDP. 2,279 were homeless. Due to very high price of land, it is very difficult for the poor to buy land and build houses. Unemployment was another problem. There were thousands of unemployed people in the Panchayat. They lived on the meagre income from part-time jobs. Women were paid less than men for the same kind of work. Many women were employed as housemaids in the urban areas. Very often they were exploited in many ways.

The total population of SCs was estimated at 3905 and they lived in 13 authorized SC colonies in different parts of the Panchayat. There were 447 families in these colonies. More than 80 per cent of the SC population were in the below poverty line (BPL) category. Drinking water problem was crucial in SC colonies. In Karakulam, more funds were spent in social sector in all the four years under study.

Table 3.19 provides the break up of spending in various sectors during 1997-98, 1998-99, 1999-2000 and 2000-01. During the first year of PCDP, 19.78 per cent went for the productive sectors. Social sector received 55.21 per cent. Spending on infrastructure projects was 15.97 per cent. SC/ST development sector received 9.05 per cent of the total amount spent during the year. In the first year of PCDP, Karakulam spent more for projects implemented in social sector. Projects in productive sector were very much less when compared to social sector.

Table 3.19 : Expenditure on Projects Implemented Sectorwise Percentage in Rupees

Sector	1997-98	1998-99	1999-2000	2000-01
Productive	19.78	28.04	10.96	18.48
Social	55.21	51.57	69.55	48.15
Infrastructure	15.97	14.05	13.64	10.56
SC/ST	9.05	6.39	5.83	23.05
TOTAL	100	100	100	100

Source : Karakulam Panchayat Document on PCDP.

In the second year of People's Plan 28.04 per cent was meant for productive sector, 51.57 per cent for social sector, 14.05 per cent for infrastructure and 6.39 per cent for SC development. We can observe substantial increase of spending on productive sector, when compared to the spending in the first year. One can also notice marginal decrease in the spending on social sector. Marginal decreases can be noted in the spending in infrastructure and SC/ST development. Despite the fact of substantial increase in the spending on productive sectors, major share of the spending had been on social sector.

The third year witnessed substantial decrease in spending on productive sector (10.96 per cent) and a quantum jump in spending on social sector (69.55 per cent). The spending on infrastructure and SC development also came down during 1999-2000. In the fourth year, productive sector received 18.48 per cent, social sector received 48.15 per cent, infrastructure sector received 10.56 per cent and SC/ST development sector received 23.05 per cent. In the fourth year, spending on social sector came down substantially. At the same time dramatic increase can be noticed in SC development sector.

However, in all the four years under study, Karakulam spent more money on the social sector.

Further details of sector-wise spending are given in Table 3.20. During 1997-98 major share had gone to education (19.98). Second largest share had gone to social welfare activities (15.22 per cent). Agriculture sector stands in the third position with 12.65 per cent. Then comes Housing with 11.64 per cent. During the first year women development (0.36 per cent) and industrial development (0.15 per cent) received very little amount despite the fact that these are two priority areas identified by the State Planning Board. During this period energy sector received 7.96 per cent, animal husbandry 6.98 per cent and drinking water projects 5.78 per cent.

In the year 1998-99 major share had gone to housing projects (19.8 per cent). Second largest spending is on social welfare sector (14.13 per cent). The third largest share had gone to animal husbandry (13.5 per cent). Industry also received substantial spending (12.3 per cent) during 1998-99. This time SC development received only 6.39 percentage. The least spending had been on women development sector (0.32 per cent). Agriculture sector also received only very little amount (2.97 per cent).

Table 3.20 : Expenditure on Projects Implemented – Sector wise details Percentage in Rupees

Sector	1997-98	1998-99	1999-2000	2000-01
Agriculture	12.65	2.24	2.97	5.95
Animal Husbandry	6.98	13.5	4.86	11.1
Industry	0.15	12.3	3.13	1.43
Infrastructure	8.01	9.28	4.32	10.56
Energy	7.96	4.77	9.32	Nil
Education	19.9	10.13	4.43	25.78
Health	2.31	4.03	38.28	6.05
Drinking water	5.78	3.16	Nil	0.22
Housing	11.64	19.8	26.84	16.1
Social Welfare	15.22	14.13	Nil	Nil
Women Development	0.36	0.32	Nil	Nil
SC/ST	9.05	6.39	5.83	23.05
TOTAL	100.00	100.00	100.00	100.00

Source : Karakulam Panchayat Document on PCDP.

During 1999-2000 health sector received maximum amount (38.28 per cent). Housing sector emerged as the second largest sector with a spending of Rs.26.84. Energy projects received 9.32 per cent. Absolutely no amount had been spent for women development during 1999-2000. SC sector received 5.83 per cent.

Projects in education sector received maximum amount during 2000-01 (25.78 per cent). Another important area that received more funding is infrastructure development (10.56 per cent). SC/ST developments received 23.05 per cent during 2000-01. No projects were implemented in women development sector. Industry received 1.43 per cent.When all the four years taken together agriculture sector received only very little. It was 12.65 per cent in the first year. In the second year it drastically came down to 2.24 per cent. In the third year the spending on agriculture was 2.97 per cent and in the fourth year it increased slightly to 5.95 per cent. Animal husbandry received substantial spending only in the second year. Industry also received attention only in the second year. In all the four years major portion of the amount went for projects in education and housing sectors. Women development projects received very little amount in the first two years. Table 4.2

reveals that no amount was spent on this sector during the third and fourth year. SC development received only scant attention in the first three years. However in the fourth year substantial amount had been spent for the development of SCs.

Let us now have a look at the sector-wise details of the projects implemented in all the four years. This would help us to understand the nature and quality of the projects implemented and the physical achievements obtained as a result of implementation of these projects.

Table 3.21 provides the details of the projects implemented in the productive sector during 1997-98. A total of ten projects were

Table 3.21 : Expenditure on Projects completed in Productive Sector in 1997-98

Sl. No.	Name of project	Expenditure (in Rs.)	%	Achievements
1.	Extension of paddy cultivation	1,07,410	6.48	Extended to 10.23 hectares
2.	Vegetable cultivation production increased	1,55,831	9.40	Vegetable backyards of 6742 houses brought under vegetable cultivation
3.	Banana cultivation	46,600	2.99	100 units started
4.	Coconut cultivation	43,467	2.62	4937 new coconuts planted
5.	Betel leaf cultivation	62,293	3.76	Encouragement has been given to 130 units
6.	Cattle-rearing	1,36,608.00	8.24	60 kg feeding materials have been given to 98 cattles
7.	Backyard Poultry farm	83,100	5.01	831 families received. 5 chickens are given
8.	Poultry club in school	20,000	1.21	200 school children received 2 chickens each
9.	Rabies controlling programme	91,547	5.52	600 dogs vaccinated
10.	Reed production Unit	10,000	.60	Capital is given to reed industry
	TOTAL	16,56,856	100.00	

Source : Karakulam Panchayat Document on PCDP.

implemented during this period by spending Rs.16,56,856. Agricultural projects included extension of paddy cultivation, vegetable cultivation, banana, coconut and betel leaf cultivation. Major portion of the spending had gone to vegetable cultivation and extension of paddy cultivation. Backyards of 6742 houses were brought under vegetable cultivation and this has contributed substantially to the increase in vegetable production. Paddy project achieved the extension of paddy cultivation to 10.23 hectres. Hundred banana cultivation units were started by spending Rs.46,600. 4937 new coconut saplings were planted by spending an amount of Rs.43,467. Cattle rearing, backyard poultry farm and poultry clubs in schools were the projects implemented in the animal husbandry sector. Cattle rearing project spent Rs.1,36,608 for the purchase and supply of 60 kg of feeding materials to 98 cattles. 831 families received 5 chickens each for developing backyard poultry farm. 200 school children received two chickens each through the school poultry clubs. For rabies control Rs.91,547 had been spent and 600 dogs vaccinated.

In the industry sector Rs.10,000 had been spent for starting a reed production unit.

Table 3.22 shows the projects implemented in social sector during 1997-98. Total 20 projects were implemented by spending Rs.42,45,816. Rs.1,58,547 had been spend for a project named mother-child care project. The physical achievement of the project is the establishment of feeding centres for children. Rs. 7,87,300 had been spent for construction of 793 latrines. The major project of the year was housing scheme for which Rs. 8,00,000 had been spent. The achievement of the project is 33 houses for the poor. By spending Rs. 87,190 a library maintenance project was implemented. Three libraries in the Panchayat benefited out of the project. By spending Rs.50,397, resource maps were prepared with people's participation.

A training camp for *Ayalkootam* convenors had been organised by spending Rs.25,000. Fifty families received financial assistance for thatching of roofs. 76 drinking water wells were dug by spending Rs.2,34,202. Poor school children in the Panchayat were supplied with school uniform. 234 students benefited out of this project by incurring an expenditure of Rs.45,000. Three hundred kerosene stoves were distributed among the poor by spending Rs.45,000.

Table 3.22 : Expenditure on Projects completed in Social Sector in 1997-98

Sl. No.	Name of project	Expenditure (in Rs.)	%	Achievements
1.	Mother-child care project	1,58,547	27.28	In feeding centres milk was given to them
2.	Latrine construction	7,87,300	18.54	393 latrines were completed
3.	Housing	8,00,500	18.85	33 houses were completed
4.	Library maintenance	87,190	2.05	Development of Panchayat library; 2 other libraries received Rs. 5000/ for purchasing books
5.	Resources mapping	50,397	1.18	With great public participation map completed
6.	Women's awareness	25,000	.59	Training for ayalkoottam camp conveners and other ladies on different projects
7.	Thatching of roof	25,000	.59	Financial aid is given to 50 families
8.	Drinking water wells	2,34,202	5.52	76 wells were constructed
9.	Smokeless chullah	9,000	.21	Money deposited with ANERT
10.	Uniform for poor children	46,768	1.10	234 students benefited
11.	Kerosine stove	45,000	.06	Distributed 300 kerosene stoves
12.	Integrated dry land financial assistance cultivation	4,54,235	10.7	For Intercrops
13.	Computer centre	7,61,398	17.93	Computer centre established in rural resource centre
14.	Milch cow	1,21,295	2.86	Cattle feed of 90 kg supplied to 138 milch cows for 3 months
15.	Veterinary services	27,450	.65	Basic facilities improved
16	Kundiricakuzhy drinking water scheme	2,80,499	6.61	
17	Kunnorkal drinking water scheme	50,000	1.18	
18	Rural resource centre	2,70,160	6.36	
19	Venkode L.P. School	5,875	.14	Basic amenities improved
20	Kazhunad L.P. School	6000	.14	Basic amenities improved
	TOTAL	42,45,816	100.00	

Source : Karakulam Panchayat Document on PCDP.

Rs.9,000 towards the purchase of smokeless chullah. Financial assistance to the tune of Rs. 4,54,235 had been provided for the promotion of intercrops. The name of the project is integrated dry land cultivation. A rural resource centre had been established by spending Rs.7,61,398. Cattle feed of 90 kg was supplied to 138 milch cows for three months by spending Rs.1,21,295. Two drinking water projects were also implemented during the year.

Sixteen projects were implemented in the infrastructure sector during 1997-98 (Table 3.23). Major portion of the amount spent had gone to road construction and for repair works in roads. Another substantial portion had been spent for the purchase of furniture for Panchayat community centres. Purchase of solar lanterns, supply of equipments to promote self employment among women, purchase of electric choke, etc. are the other projects included in infrastructure sector during the year.

Table 3.23 : Expenditure on Projects completed in Infrastructure Sector in 1997-98

Sl. No.	Name of project	Expenditure (in Rs.)	%	Achievements
1.	Manjamkodu IHDP community hall	1,18,000	10.35 %	Furniture purchased for community hall
2.	Chekkala Mukal Nursery	14,920	1.31 %	Purchased furniture for the nursery
3.	Energy Conservation	40,600	3.56 %	Distributed 700 CFL
4.	Kaipada Plavila road	85,990	7.54 %	NA
5.	Self-employment scheme for women	1,45,000	12.72 %	Equipments have been distributed to 50 SC women
6.	Taratta Pullikonam road	62,149	5.45 %	NA
7.	Photocopy machine	1,00,200	8.79 %	Deposited (for Panchayat use)
8.	Electronic choke for electricity Deposited money in conservation	48,300	4.24%	ANERT (consumer's constitution)
9.	Valiyavila Christ nagar road	12,000	1,05 %	NA
10.	Mulamukku Kozhryodu road	12,000	1.05 %	NA
11.	Karayalathukonam pachakadu road	30,362	2.66 %	NA
12.	Solar lantern (general)	50,000	4.38 %	100 lanterns
13.	Valiyavila Mullapura road	12,000	1.05 %	NA
14.	Enikara Njalikonam road	41,381	2.75 %	NA
15.	Electric line extension	3,54,720	31.13 %	Deposited in KSEB
16.	Mukkola Kavil road	12,000	1.05 %	NA
	TOTAL	11,39,622	100	

Source : Karakulam Panchayat Document on PCDP.

Projects completed in the SC/ST sector during 1997-98 are given in Table 3.24. On the whole six projects were implemented by spending Rs.7,07,810. Under SC development project a road had been constructed in an SC colony by spending Rs. 27,564. Three projects were implemented for the welfare of SC students. Under these projects SC students were supplied with school uniforms, study materials, tables and chairs. By spending Rs.1,45,000 fifty SC women were supplied with implements. (See Table 3.24)

Table 3.24 : Expenditure on Projects Completed in SC/ST Sector in 1997-98

Sl. No.	Name of project	Expenditure (in Rs.)	%	Achievements
1.	SC Students welfare	1,26,826	17.92	706 supplied uniforms and notebooks
2.	Uniform and study materials for SC students	1,68,420	23.79	763 SC students benefited
3.	Improvement of facilities for SC students	1,40,500	19.85	50 SC students were given table and chair
4.	Self-employment for SC women	1,45,000	20.48	50 SC women were supplied with implements
5.	Solar lantern	99,500	14.05	50 SC families benefited
6.	Chencherivila Harijan colony road	27,564	3.89	NA
	TOTAL	7,07,810	100	

Source : Karakulam Panchayat Document on PCDP.

Table 3.25 shows the projects implemented in the productive sector during 1998-99. Totally fifteen projects had been implemented by spending Rs.12,96,993. Most of the projects were similar to those implemented in the previous year. They were cattle rearing (Rs.3,05,153), milch cow rearing (Rs. 6,02,937), Pregnancy care for cows (Rs.68,420), Mini dairy unit (Rs.5512), Kamadhenu insurance (Rs.29,469), Fertility camp for cows (Rs.19,742), Rabies control (Rs.11,239), Veterinary hospital development (Rs.69,659), extension of vegetable cultivation to 3.75 acres (Rs.5,878), Banana plantation (Rs.2,975), Paddy development (Rs.52,664). Labour force development (Rs.7,825), Integrated dry land cultivation (Rs.11,645), Irrigation well (Rs. 98,000) and Rain water harvesting (Rs.5,875) were the projects implemented in productive sector during 98-99. Of these two are innovative projects. A labour force had been created by enrolling 57 agricultural workers under the project called labour force development. Another innovative project is the construction of 92 pits for rain water harvesting. These two projects are different from the routine ones which we have seen so far.

Table 3.25 : Expenditure on Projects completed in Productive Sector –1998-99

Sl. No.	Name of project	Expenditure (in Rs.)	%	Achievements
1.	Cattle rearing	3,05,153	23.53	NA
2.	Milch cow rearing	6,02,937	46.49	NA
3.	Pregnancy care for cows	68,420	5.27	NA
4.	Mini-dairy unit	5,512	.42	NA
5.	Kamadhenu insurance	29,469	2.27	NA
6.	Fertility camp for cows	19,742	1.52	NA
7.	Rabies control	11,239	.87	NA
8.	Veterinary hospital Development	69,659	5.37	NA
9.	Vegetable Development	5,878	.45	Vegetable cultivation extended to 3.75acres
10.	Banana plantation	2,975	.23	NA
11.	Paddy Development	52,664	4.06	Paddy cultivation in 8 hectares
12.	Labour force Development	7,825	.60	57 agricultural workers enrolled in to labour force
13.	Integrated dry land cultivation	11,645	.9	NA
14.	Irrigation well	98,000	7.56	Irrigation facilities for 7 acres of land
15.	Rain water harvesting	5,875	.45	92 pits constructed
	TOTAL	12,96,993	100.00	

Source : Karakulam Panchayat Document on PCDP.

Projects completed in the social sector in the year 1998-99 is given in Table 3.26. Twenty-six projects were implemented by spending Rs.37,38,835. Sizeable amount had been spent for further development of the rural resource centre. It had been developed as a computer education centre. Second major project of the year is 'Operation Olympia'. A rural sports complex had been established for the identification and the promotion of youth talent in sports activities. Similarly a 'Kalagramam' (Arts complex) had been established for the promotion of talents in arts and literature. Another important programme of the Panchayat during 98-99

Table 3.26 : Expenditure on Projects completed in the Social Sector in 1998-99

Sl. No.	Name of project	Expenditure (in Rs.)	%	Achievements
1.	Repair and maintenance of drinking water wells	15,000	.40	15 wells
2.	Ayurvedic hospital development	8757	.23	NA
3.	L.P. School-smokeless chullah	9,646	.26	NA
4.	Improving standards of Schools	28,288	.76	NA
5.	Model pre-primary school	150,000	14.76	NA
6.	Kalagramam	31,916	.85	NA
7.	Operation Olympia	1,02,268	2.73	NA
8.	Sport kit distribution	10,000	.27	NA
9.	Rural resource centre	3,14,796	8.42	NA
10.	Computer education	52,800	1.41	NA
11.	Grants for activities of rural resource centre	25,000	.67	NA
12.	Industry	10,17,008	27.20	NA
13.	Mother and child care	2,97,076	7.94	Distribution of rice, milk and gram through 15 feeding centres
14.	Urinal for Venkode UPS	13,406	.36	NA
15.	Kazhunad UPS	4,404	.12	NA
16.	Panchayat library complex	79,596	2.13	NA
17.	Drinking water wells	1,76,000	4.70	NA
18.	Kunnoorkal drinking water scheme	67,956	.18	NA
19.	Latrine	5,53,750	14.81	223 latrines constructed
20.	Roof Tiles	4,22,500	11.30	62 houses tiled
21.	Women self-help group	26,510	.71	27 societies
22.	Total housing scheme	51,227	1.37	NA
23.	Plan formulation expenditure	75,000	2	NA
24.	Karimpuvila Chirakudy drinking water scheme	2,09,704	5.61	Work in progress
25.	Kundirikakuzhy drinking water scheme	51,227	1.37	Work completed
26.	Kunnoorkal OLHS	45,000	1.20	NA
	TOTAL	37,38,835	100	

Source : Karakulam Panchayat Document on PCDP

included three drinking water projects. For mother and child care Rs. 2,97,076 had been spent. Rs. 10,17,008 had been spent for the promotion of industry. Other social sector projects included maintenance and repair works in drinking water wells, schools, hospitals, etc.

Table 3.27 : Expenditure on Projects completed in Infrastructure Sector in 1998-99

Sl. No.	Name of project	Expenditure (in Rs.)	%	Achievements
1.	Kunnuvila Thekkuvila Electric line	38,450	3.47	NA
2	Madathilnada Nilami electric line	40,000	3.62	NA
3	Peringalodu Vatakayam Electric line	39,137	3.55	NA
4.	Maruthoor Kadukkarakonam electric line	39,060	3.54	NA
5.	Punnakunnu electric line	39,750	3.60	NA
6.	Pananada Kannannikonam electric line	41,450	3.75	NA
7.	Darsan nagar madavana electric line	33,100	3.00	NA
8.	Kizhakela electric line	41,205	3.73	NA
9.	Pathiyanand kudappanavilakam electric line	47,000	4.26	NA
10.	Cherukaraveedu Aramkallu electric line	35,000	3.17	NA
11.	Mulamukku Kozhiyodu road	28,077	2.54	NA
12.	Tharattappulikonam road	30,442	2.75	NA
13.	Valiavila Christ nagar colony road	16,622	1.51	NA
14.	Chencherivila Hcroad	28,930	2.62	NA
15.	Valiavila Mullapura road	16,800	1.52	NA
16.	Karayalathukonam Pachakadu road	11,659	1.05	NA
17.	Kaipada Plavila road	53,890	4.88	NA
18.	Enikara moolanada Njalikonam road	50,279	4.56	NA
19.	Enikara Vilavuṭhottam road	9,700	.88	NA
20.	Kachani Kannamathu road	30,200	2.74	NA
21.	Kizhkallayam Kudetiela road	47,963	4.35	NA
22.	Plakkotu Kunnumpuram road	12,000	1.1	NA
23.	Kaipada plavuvila road	42,000	3.81	NA
24.	Theepachivila road	10,000	.91	NA
25.	Venkodu pezhumoodu road	7,500	.68	NA
26.	Kunnoorkal laksham veedu road	10,000	.91	NA
27	Attaravattom Kizhakela road	10,000	.91	NA
28	Karakulam bridge	2,66,000	24.11	NA
29	Repairwork at Vattapara PHC	27,000	2.45	NA
	TOTAL	11,03,214	100	

Source : Karakulam Panchayat Document on PCDP.

Twenty-eight projects were implemented in infrastructure sector during 1998-99 by spending Rs.11,03,214. Of this ten projects were in the power sector. Money had been spent for the extension of electric lines to the interior areas of the Panchayat where electricity did not reach till then. All other projects were in road sector—construction of new roads, repair of existing ones, construction of culverts etc.

Four projects had been implemented in the Panchayat for SC/ST development by spending Rs.5,27,750. Substantial portion of this amount had been spent for housing development and latrine construction. 28 latrines had been completed by spending Rs.68,750. Rs. 32,000 had been spent for the computer education of SC students.

Table 3.28 : Expenditure on Projects completed in SC/ST Sector in 1998-99

Sl. No.	Name of project	Expenditure (in Rs.)	%	Achievements
1.	Latrine	68,750	13.03	28 latrines completed
2.	Thekuvila lakshamveedu (housing)	3,48,000	65.94	NA
3.	Housing	79,000	14.97	NA
4.	Computer education	32,000	6.06	NA
	TOTAL	5,27,750	100	

Source : Karakulam Panchayat Document on PCDP.

Table 3.29 shows the amount spent in the productive sector during 1999-2000. In this year five projects had been implemented. Two projects had been implemented in the agriculture sector. Rs. 1,32,256 had been spent for integrated paddy development. For integrated dry land cultivation Rs.34,580 had been spent. A project called integrated animal husbandry had been implemented during the year by spending Rs. 3,64,671. Under the project cattle rearing stables, poultry units and piggeries were started. 700 domestic dogs were vaccinated. For the development of industry Rs.2,35,000 had been spent. This amount had been spent for the purchase of land for the establishment of an industrial cooperative society. Also, preliminary works had been completed for the establishment of copra processing units.

Table 3.29 : Expenditure on Projects completed in Productive Sector in 1999-2000

Sl. No.	Name of project	Expenditure (in Rs.)	%	Achievements
1.	Integrated paddy development	1,32,256	16.1	44.2 tonne paddy in the first harvest and 31.9 tonne paddy in the second harvest
2.	Integrated dry land cultivation	34,580	4.2	Intercrop cultivation
3.	Labour force	55,920	6.8	Harvest machine purchased
4.	Integrated animal husbandry	3,64,671	44.3	Dairy development, cattle rearing, stable renovation, 230 poultry units, piggery and 700 domestic dogs were vaccinated
5.	Industry	2,35,000	28.5	Land purchased for industrial cooperative society; preliminary works completed for the establishment of copra processing unit
	TOTAL	8,22,427	100	

Source : Karakulam Panchayat Document on PCDP.

In the year 1999-2000, four projects had been completed in the social sector by spending Rs.52,15,474. The first project is named 'Integrated Education Programme'. Rs. 2,53,667 had been spent for the implementation of this project. Physical achievements of this project include the following: (1) Children's festival, (2) Special coaching for SSLC students, (3) Arts village, (4) Pre-primary development, (5) Documentation centre and (6)Technical education development.

Secondly, under the 'Operation Olympia' project, 50 students were given training in sports and games by spending Rs.78,791. The name of the third project is 'Total Health Programme'. Under this

Rs.28,70,516 had been spent for constructing latrines and for free supply of gram, rice and milk for the poorer sections in the Panchayat. The most important project of the year is 'Total Housing Scheme'. Rs.20,12,500 had been spent for constructing houses. This project had been implemented to provide on dwelling unit to all houseless families in the Panchayat.

Table 3.30 : Expenditure on Projects Completed in Social Sector in 1999-2000

Sl. No.	Name of project	Expenditure (in Rs.)	%	Achievements
1.	Integrated education Children's festival; special programme	2,53,667	4.8	Coaching for SSLC students, arts village pre-primary, documentation, technical education
2.	Operation Olympia	78,791	1.5	50 students were given training in sports and games
3.	Total Health Programme	28,70,516	55.1	Rise, gram and milk distributed; latrine for all houses
4.	Total Housing Scheme	20,12,500	38.5	House for everyone in the Panchayat
	TOTAL	52,15,474	100.00	

Source : Karakulam Panchayat Document on PCDP

During the same year Rs. 10,23,000 had been spent for completion of projects in the infrastructure sector. Road construction in several areas of the Panchayat continued during 1999-2000 also. Rs.2,24,000 had been spent for road development. For establishing notice boards in important locations in the Panchayat Rs.1,00,000 had been spent. Under the energy management project 70 CFL lamps had been purchased and distributed. During this year only one project had been completed in the SC/ST development sector by spending Rs.4,37,500. Three cents of land for each landless SC had been purchased for house construction.

Table 3.31 : Expenditure on Projects completed in Infrastructure Sector in 1999-2000

Sl. No.	Name of project	Expenditure (in Rs.)	%	Achievements
1.	Energy management	6,99,000	68.3	700 CFL
2.	Notice Board	1,00,000	9.8	86 notice boards were established in all important junctions of the Panchayat
3.	Transport	2,24,000	21.9	Roads construction in several area of the Panchayat continues
	TOTAL	10,23,000	100	

Source : Karakulam Panchayat Document on PCDP.

Table 3.32 : Expenditure on Projects Completed in SC/ST Sector in 1999-2000

Sl. No.	Name of project	Expenditure (in Rs.)	%	Achievements
1.	Housing scheme for the landless SCs	4,37,500		3 cents of land has been purchased for the landless SCs for house construction
	TOTAL	4,37,500		

Source : Karakulam Panchayat Document on PCDP.

During 2000-01, 8 projects had been implemented in the productive sector. Integrated paddy development project, integrated dry land cultivation project, animal husbandry projects and projects for the development of industry in the Panchayat had been implemented during the year. Extension of paddy cultivation area, construction of drinking water well, banana cultivation, coconut development, ginger and turmeric cultivation, tuber crops cultivation, etc. found place in the list of achievements in agriculture sector during the year. Animal husbandry sector witnessed establishment of dairy units, poultry unit and rabbit unit. Money had been spent for rabies control also.One electronic training and production unit had been established during 2000-01. Building construction started; computer and computer peripherals had been purchased.

Table 3.33 : Expenditure on Projects completed in the Productive Sector in 2000-2001

Sl. No.	Name of project	Expenditure (in Rs.)	%	Achievements
1	Integrated paddy development	40,607	1.23	Assistance for paddy development in 4.5 hectares.
2	Integrated dry land cultivation	1,63,030	4.95	Drinking water wells (3 Nos) Banana cultivation as inter crop in 3.14 hectares of coconut estate; .61 hectares ginger and turmeric cultivation as inter crop; .86 hectares tuber crops.
3.	Integrated dry land cultivation	2,76,638	8.41	606 coconut saplings distributed;banana cultivation as inter-crop in 6.7 hectors of coconutestate; ginger, turmeric cultivation as in 1.5 hector; 1.18 hector tuber crops.
4.	Animal husbandry	4,41,119	13.41	Dairy development; cattle rearing; mini dairy unit
5.	Animal husbandry	4,62,002	14.04	Rabies control vaccination for domestic dogs; dairy development poultry development; rabbit unit
6.	Industry	76,493	2.32	Building construction started
7.	Industry	40,000	1.21	Building construction
8.	Electronic training and production	17,89,950	54.41	Building construction; purchase of computer and computer peripherals
	TOTAL	32,89,839	100	

Source : Karakulam Panchayat Document on PCDP.

Rs.21,42,409 had been spent in social sector during 2000-01. On the whole six projects were implemented. All the six were the continuation of the projects started in the previous year. Physical achievements of the projects include the following:

(1) 503 school children were given computer education; special coaching had been arranged for students appearing for the SSLC examination.

(2) Basic amenities provided in schools by spending Rs.40,000.

(3) Under 'operation Olympia' 50 students were given coaching in sports and games; uniforms and nutrient foods were supplied to sports students

(4) Under integrated health development programme 125 mothers and 425 children were given milk and noon meal for 25 days and 20 days respectively. Status of women survey and health survey conducted. For this Rs.4,93,816 had been spent.

Finally, under the Thanal housing scheme Rs.13,14,050 had been spent for providing houses to 250 families.

Table 3.34 : Expenditure on Projects Completed in Social Sector in 2000-01

Sl. No.	Name of project	Expenditure (in Rs.)	%	Achievements
1.	Education programme	1,01,719	4.7	503 school children were given computer education; coaching for SSLC students.
2.	Basic amenities in Schools	40,000	1.86	Basic facilities provided
3.	Operation Olympia	1,73,727	8.11	50 students were given coaching in sports and games; uniforms and nutrient food were supplied to sports students
4.	Integrated health programme	4,93,816	23.05	125 mothers and 425 children were given milk and noon-meal for 25 days and 20 days respectively; status of women survey, health survey
5.	Kunnorkal drinking water project	18,097	.84	Project completed
6.	Thanal housing scheme	13,15,050	61.38	250 people were provided with houses
	TOTAL	21,42,409	100	

Source : Karakulam Panchayat Document on PCDP.

Projects completed in the infrastructure sector during 2000-01 is given in Table 3.35. Rs. 8,43,742 had been spent during the year for the completion of 15 projects.

Table 3.35 : Expenditure on Projects completed in Infrastructure Sector in 2000-01

Sl. No.	Name of project	Expenditure (in Rs.)	%	Achievements
1.	Plan formulation and monitoring	1,32,306	15.7	NA
2.	Mukkambalamoodu Panthalakodu road	68,611	8.1	220 m road tarred
3.	Vettikodam madavana road	19,737	2.3	220 m road completed
4.	Enikara Kannanikonam road	68,903	8.2	1600 m work completed
5.	Kunnorkal laksham veedu Valiyavila road	19,500	2.3	Work in progress
6.	Karakulam Punnoor road	129,000	3.4	Work in progress
7.	Kallayam kazhinad road	14,914	1.7	40 m side wall; 30 m mud filling; work completed
8.	Thsaratta pazhayattin-kara road	67,470	7.9	220 m work completed
9.	Pothod Manjamcodu road	36,047	4.3	150 m work completed
10.	Aruviyodu St.Rita's-Kaippada road 9	0,335	10.7	250m work completed
11.	Melamcode road	47,000	5.6	1km road completed
12.	Paravoorkonam road	46,656	5.5	2km road completed
13.	Kizhakela Edacod road	68,253	8.1	100 m completed
14.	Pallivila Njattadivaram road	68,945	8.2	Road concreting 50 m
15.	Kodoor pezhummood road	66,065	7.8	75 m road completed
	TOTAL	8,43,742	100	

Source : Karakulam Panchayat Document on PCDP.

All the fifteen projects had been implemented for road development. The works carried out included road tarring, concreting, mud filling, etc.

Two projects had been implemented for SC development during the year (Table 3.36). First project is land for the landless. Under this project, 54 SC families had been provided with 5 cents of land. For this Rs.8,94,250 had been spent. The second project is Thanal housing scheme. Under this project Rs.98,950 had been spent for house construction. One hundred and eleven SC families benefited out of this project.

Table 3.36 : Expenditure on Projects Completed in SC/ST Sector in 2000-01

Sl. No.	Name of project	Expenditure (in Rs.)	%	Achievements
1	Land for landless SCs	8,94,250	54	SC families were provided with 3 cent of land
2	Thanal housing scheme	9,88,500		Panchayat's share for Thanal scheme has been given to 100 SC families; 35,000 each were given to 3 SC families; 5000 each were given to 8 SC families as additional financial assistance for house construction
	TOTAL	18,82,750		

Source : Karakulam Panchayat Document on PCDP.

Nutritional foods were distributed to mothers and children through 13 feeding centres and two nurseries. In the health sector during 1999-2000 Rs.73,000 was spent for completing the construction of Primary Health Centre at a place by name Vattappara. Making the PHC as a model one was the objective behind the construction work undertaken. During 1999-2000 with the help of District and Block Panchayat, the Panchayat had undertaken construction of 300 houses in the Panchayat with a view to make available dwelling units to all the families without a house.

Respective Gram Sabhas had identified beneficiaries for the housing scheme. Social Sector received good attention in the first year (1997-98) also. During 1997-98, 55.21 per cent was the actual amount spent for this sector. During this period in social sector education received more attention. The total spending on education in 1997-98 was 19.9 per cent. Rural Library development, resource mapping, uniform for poor school children, establishment of a rural resource centre with computer facilities are the works undertaken during this period. Improving infrastructure facilities like construction of urinals for schools were other projects implemented in education sector during 1997-98. During the same period three drinking water schemes were initiated. Housing and other social welfare activities also received attention the first year of people's plan.

During 1998-99 social sector spending was to the tune of 51.57 per cent. Education received 10.13 per cent. Housing received 19.8 per cent. Other social welfare activities combined together received 14.13 per cent. Apart from spending for providing basic amenities to schools in the Panchayat, major portion of the money went for further strengthening of the rural resource and study centre.

In the fourth year of people's plan, spending in social sector was comparatively less (48.15 per cent). Of this major share had gone to education (25.78 per cent). Second largest share had been to housing. In education sector major share was spent for developing students' abilities in sports. The project was named 'Operation Olympia'. Second largest priority areas were computer literacy for school children. However, top most priority had gone to construction of building for electronic training and production centre attached to the rural resource and study centre.

Compared to social sector spending, what had gone to productive sector is unimpressive. The highest percentage (28.04) of spending was in the year 1998-99. Major share of spending was on animal husbandry. Industry received only scant attention. Spending on agriculture is also not impressive. In 1997-98 agriculture sector received 12.65 per cent. However in subsequent years, the spending got reduced sizably.

III

In the preceding sections, development projects implemented by the Panchayats under study have been analysed with a view to understand the utility and reliability of decentralised approach for petty production sector and quality improvement in basic services like education and health. In the next chapter we will have a look at the role of Gram Sabha in participatory democracy and development.

4

DEMOCRACY AND DEVELOPMENT AT THE LOCAL LEVEL

The Role of Gram Sabha

People's Assembly (Gram Sabha) at the local level as an instrument of direct democracy had its roots in the Indian tradition. This traditional instrument of democracy got a prominent place in the Gandhian concept of self-sufficient village republic. However, the constitution makers of India could not accommodate this Gandhian ideal in its proper place due to Ambedkar's reservation about traditional villages. He felt that revival of traditional village Panchayats with constitutional protection would lead to obscurantism of the upper castes in the rural areas. Therefore, the entire subject of Panchayat Raj institutions and local level democracy had been relegated to non-justiciable position by including it in part four of the Indian Constitution, the directive principles of state policy. Even then Gram Sabhas got a place in the local body acts of many states. The Panchayat Raj Acts of Uttar Pradesh and Bihar contained provisions for constituting Gram Sabhas. Rajasthan also experimented with Gram Sabha during the time of the first generation of Panchayat Raj institutions in India. All these earlier attempts to constitute Gram Sabhas miserably failed. In 1962 the Government of India appointed a committee headed by R.R Diwakar to study about the Gram Sabhas and to put forward suggestions to make it a device of true democracy at the local level. The committee under the chairmanship of the veteran Gandhian made the following observation:

"Our experience is that even in those states where the institution of Gram Sabha has been introduced by statutes as early as 1947, it cannot be said that the institution has been functioning there in any real sense of the term. Generally these Gram Sabha meetings are thinly attended and a quorum is seldom achieved" (Government of India, 1963).

The Committee also identified the factors that contributed to the failure of Gram Sabhas:

1. Lack of awareness among the village regarding the functions of Gram Sabha.

2. Personal nature of village politics.

3. Absence of a common or appropriate venue for the meetings.

4. Selection of inappropriate times for the meetings.

5. Inadequate publicity given to the meeting.

6. Reluctance of Pradhan of the Panchayat to convene the meeting.

7. Apathy of the villages. (*ibid.*)

Diwakar Committee recommended a gradualist approach to the whole issue of strengthening of Gram Sabhas. The committee was not at all against Gram Sabha. But it took the position that strengthening of Panchayat should precede any attempt at constituting of Gram Sabha.

The cherished ideal of Gram Sabha which was a 'non-starter' earlier got a coveted position in the new Panchayati Raj System with the enactment of the 73rd and 74th Amendments to the Constitution of India. As per the 73rd amendment Gram Sabhas were envisaged as the bottom layer of the three-tier Panchayat Raj institutions. In urban areas ward committees were suggested as per the 74th Amendment Act.

Constitutional Validity of Gram Sabha
73rd Amendment Act, 1992
Part IX

According to Article 243(b) of the Indian Constitution Gram Sabha means a body consisting of persons registered in the electoral rolls relating to a village comprised within the area of Panchayat at the village level.

In Article 243-A Gram Sabha may exercise such power and perform such functions at the village level as the legislature of a state may, by law provide.

Constitutional Validity of Ward Committees
74th Amendment Act, 1992
Part IX-A

1. There shall be constituted ward committees consisting of one or more wards within the territorial area of a Municipality having a population of 3 lakhs or more.

2. The Legislature of a State may by law make provisions with respect to

a. The composition and territorial area of a ward committee.

b. The manner in which the seats in a ward committee shall be filled.

3. A member of Municipality representing a ward within the territorial area of the ward committee shall be a member of the committee.

4. Where a ward committee consists of

(a) One ward, the member representing that ward in the Municipality, or

(b) Two or more wards, one of the members representing such wards in the Municipality elected by the members of the ward committee shall be the chairperson of that committee.

Nothing in this article shall be deemed to prevent the Legislature of a State from making any provision for the constitution of committees in addition to the ward committees.

The 73rd Amendment to the Constitution provided the over all framework of Gram Sabha and the State Legislatures were given the freedom to determine the powers and functions of Gram Sabhas in respective States. As a result of this, the powers and functions of Gram Sabhas are different in various States in India. However, in almost all States Gram Sabhas exist only in theory. A study conducted by Society for Participatory Research in Asia (PRIA) in six states in 1997 revealed that the minimum required quorum was rarely fulfilled and "records of Gram Sabha meetings were completed even when either meetings were not held or quorums were not completed". The exception to this general trend is West Bengal where Gram Sabhas have been given a prominent place in suggesting proposals for public works and monitoring the activities of LSGIs (Isaac, 2000).

Based on the framework of legislations at the Centre, the Government of Kerala had also initiated and gave shape to a legislation called Kerala Panchayati Raj Act, 1994.

Section 3 of the second chapter of the Kerala Panchayati Raj Act, 1994 deals with the structure and other details of Gram Sabhas in Kerala.

1. Each Mandalam (ward) of a village Panchayat shall be considered as a village for the formation of Gram Sabha.

2. At the village level Gram Sabha shall be constituted consisting of persons belonging to the territorial area of village Panchayat as well as registered in the electoral roll of the village.

3. Gram Sabhas must be convened minimum twice in a year in a place decided by the village Panchayat. (As per Sen Committee recommendation, the Act was amended and meeting of Gram Sabhas should be convened four times a year.)

4. The ward member who represents the constituency which comes under the territorial area of village shall be the convenor of the particular Gram Sabha. Due to any reasons, if he is not able to perform his duties physically or by some other constraints, the ward member who is representing the nearest ward shall be appointed as the convenor.

5. The president of the village Panchayat shall preside over all the meetings of Gram Sabha. In his absence the vice president shall preside and if both of them are absent, the convenor of the Gram Sabha shall preside over the function.

6. The village Panchayat shall have to place the reports of the developmental programmes conducted during the previous year pertaining to that constituency, the developmental programmes that are expected to be under taken during the current year and it

expected expenditure, a statement of the annual expenditure and a report of the administration in the first meeting of the Gram Sabha.

If any of the decisions of the Gram Sabha fails to be implemented under any circumstances, the person who presides over the meeting shall have report the reasons in the Gram Sabha.

7. If there are any recommendations or suggestions from the Gram Sabha then the District Panchayat, Block Panchayat and Gram Panchayat shall have to give genuine consideration.

8. Gram Sabhas have to perform the various functions such as:

(a) To render help in preparing developmental schemes for the villages and encourage it. To supervise (monitor and evaluate) the implementation of developmental programmes.

(b) To foster a sense of unity and harmony among the different groups of people.

(c) To mobilize voluntary work (shramadan), to collect money or things in the form of donation for social welfare programmes.

(d) To help in the implementation of developmental schemes pertaining to the village.

(e) To help in identifying the beneficiaries for the developmental programmes and welfare schemes pertaining to the village.

(f) To discuss the suggestions for the implementation of the literacy programmes and to help in the implementation process.

(g) Other functions as provided (specified).

(h) To conduct discussions about the reports mentioned in the sub-section 6 and about the various developmental activities. To submit suggestions and recommendations about the developmental activities.

9. The procedures for convening and conducting Gram Sabhas must be provided (specified).

10. The quorum of the Gram Sabha must not be less than 50 (Amended as 10 per cent of electorate or 100 persons).

11. Resolutions shall be passed in the Gram Sabha meeting on a majority basis on any problem which comes under the jurisdiction of the Gram Sabha.

There are four main items in the rules and regulations of Gram Sabha. They are—

1. The Gram Sabha meetings must be conducted between 8 AM. and 6 PM.

2. The date, time and venue of the Gram Sabha meetings must be displayed in common places, Government offices, schools and village/Panchayat offices.

3. The Secretary of the Village Panchayat in consultation with the President must prepare a programme schedule which includes the matters to be discussed in the Gram Sabha.

4. The resolution which are passed on a majority basis in the Gram Sabha shall be informed to the concerned Panchayat within a week.

The 73rd and 74th Constitutional Amendments wanted that the LSGIs should be involved in planning. For that purpose a new structure, the District Planning Committee was mandated to be formed in every district.

The State Planning Board wanted to utilize the Local Bodies Act to implement its decentralised planning. It was decided to make use of the Gram Sabhas as the mass base for implementing the programme of local level planning. As has already been mentioned the first step in local level planning is the identification of felt needs of the people in the locality. Mobilisation of people in a massive way is required to identify the 'felt-needs' of the people. There fore the first phase of the campaign started with three objectives and concentrating on activating Gram Sabhas.

Special Gram Sabhas for People's Planning – Their Practical Viability

There existed wide spread scepticism about the practical feasibility of Gram Sabhas. How far it is practical and to what extent it can act as a device of direct democracy and participatory planning. Unfortunately an indifferent attitude developed in general about organizing of special Gram Sabhas for implementing decentralised planning. It was widely felt that there would be over crowding of people in the Gram Sabhas.

Each Gram Sabha in Kerala has 1500-2000 members approximately. Many of the Panchayats do not have sufficiently big halls to conduct the Gram Sabha meetings. Another problem was that useful discussions with active participation were not possible among a people's gathering like this. To a certain extent all these doubts were genuine. But could these doubts be the exclusive reason for the indifferent attitude and dislike towards the Gram Sabhas? Some local leaders could not digest the process in which people take stock of the activities of the elected representatives of the local self-government institutions. Some people expressed doubts about the practical viability of the concept of social auditing. All these doubts when considered in the context of the style of political functioning in the State could not be ignored. At the same time, it was felt that if Gram Sabhas were conducted properly, they could be used as a pulsating and vibrant instrument to narrow down the ever widening gap between people and administration. Gram Sabhas could be instrumental in mobilizing resources as well as voluntary work for the developmental activities of the Panchayat. Gram Sabha could play a pivotal role in enlisting and evoking people's participation as well as in motivating and stimulating people's support. Gram Sabhas could be used as effective agents to instill and imbibe a new spirit of the development culture.

The left government wanted that Gram Sabhas must be the experimental forums for new political, social, economic and cultural development. Gram Sabhas must be an aggregation or fellowship of people beyond political affiliations and party allegiance. The Panchayat committee and the political parties which represent the majority of the people (local leadership) had to take the initiative for the smooth functioning of Gram Sabhas. They had to create a harmonious and congenial working environment in Gram Sabhas where direct democracy could not be masked. The representatives of the minorities, people from the weaker sections and depressed classes should be given due importance and their genuine suggestions and opinions should be considered. Planning Board wanted to orient

Gram Sabhas in such a direction that a non-partisan platform is created to take care of development works in the locality.

Practical Viability of Gram Sabhas

Unfortunately there existed an indifferent attitude towards the convening of Gram Sabhas in the earlier days just after the 73rd Amendment and the legislation of the conformity Acts. People in some Gram Sabhas did not have an emotional attachment among them due to the artificial division of wards. The probability of huddle of people in Gram Sabhas is viewed as one of the most important problems in convening Gram Sabhas. Most of the elected representatives of the Panchayat were viewing the Gram Sabhas as an unavoidable menace since it is a mandatory provision as per the new local body Acts. This type of attitude was evident in the Gram Sabhas convened just after the 73rd Amendment and the enactment of the conformity Act in the state. The Gram Sabhas were convened out of constitutional compulsion. It recorded people's participation only to the minimum level of quorum. But things were different in the case of Gram Sabhas conducted after the people's campaign for Ninth plan as part of the people's planning process. There was definitely a change in the perspectives, attitudes and approaches of the people as well as the leadership. The Planning Board was trying to instill a new development culture in the minds of the people.

Gram Sabhas are the most appropriate channels in paving the foundation for people's planning and creating a popular base for that among the people. The main aim of decentralising power is to provide maximum opportunities to the common man for active participation in planning as well as administrative processes. This is the brightest side of democracy, which was made possible through the institutionalisation of Gram Sabha. On the other hand democracy has been reduced to a state of affairs, where people think that it is only a right to elect their representatives once in five years. Democracy guarantees not only the right to vote, *i.e.* political equality but also ensures social justice and economic equality. Real democracy is moulded and takes its true shape, when the people's ability to take decisions regarding their daily life on their own is enhanced.

In the light of the above mentioned factors, one can infer that there are barriers for decentralisation not only at the central level but at the local levels also. Everyone's interest is to have decentralisation ended with their own level.

But in the people's campaign for Ninth Plan, Gram Sabhas were given a prominent place. This is not only due to the fact that it is being guaranteed in the Constitution but also for a planning process with transparency and people's participation.

This is the approach of the people's planning process. The actively functioning Gram Sabhas provide guarantee to the effect that the elected local level leadership would not misuse power. Also, Gram Sabhas can play a more important role in programme implementation than the planning processes. The functioning of Gram Sabhas in the planning process would enable the Gram Sabhas to meet further challenges in programme implementation.

The campaign activists thought of activating the Gram Sabha by mobilising people in large numbers. They had identified that two major sets of hurdles in the way of effective participation of the people. These two constraints which were identified by plan activists were the following:

1. Lack of awareness among the people regarding the functions and powers of Gram Sabhas.
2. The appropriate location, timing and other preparatory matters were not properly organised.

To overcome these difficulties, the Planning Board had adopted certain strategies: Print and electronic media had been effectively used to create awareness among the people about the Gram Sabhas. In addition to newspaper articles and advertisements, radio talks and television spots, the following activities were suggested to be undertaken in each local body:

1. A convention of the representatives of all the political parties and mass organisations may be called to discuss the Gram Sabhas. If necessary the Panchayat/Municipal Council may create a special organizing committee with equal representation of all the political parties for organising the Gram Sabhas.

2. Separate meetings of women's organisations may be organised. Similar meetings may be held for other sections of people.

3. Special attention must be paid for participation of *Dalits.* A meeting of the community leaders may be organised.

4. Propaganda through official machinery like *Anganwadis,* PHC, and veterinary hospitals may be organised.

5. Posters and exhibitions may be put up.

6. Given the universal schooling in Kerala, announcements in school assemblies and special educational programme such as quizzes for children would be appropriate.

7. Musical performances, street theatre presentations, *Padayatra* (Processions) through the Panchayats, and traditional drum announcements may be effectively employed to draw people into the spirit of participation.

A three-hour programme was prepared with poetry, music and theatre performances on the theme "power to the people". About 1000 artists were trained and they were divided into 100 troops and they performed in several thousand locations throughout Kerala. The performance was named as "Power to-the-people-theatrical procession".

In the matter of venue and timing, following instructions were given by the Planning Board:

1. The Gram Sabha must be organized on holidays rather than on working days and the ideal time would be in the afternoon, particularly to encourage women's participation.

2. The village school was found to be an ideal location. The Gram Sabha may also be convened in public places with sufficient shade for group meetings.

3. The decision on venue and time of the meeting had to be communicated through squads that would visit every house and distribute a printed invitation.

Prior to the convening of Gram Sabha meetings, 373 volunteers at the state level and 10,863 volunteers at the district level were trained as facilitators.

How to make Gram Sabhas efficient?

Mainly three questions cropped up in connection with this.

1. How to conduct Gram Sabhas in the case of over crowding?

2. What has to be discussed in these special Gram Sabhas or what is their function?

3. How to conduct these discussions? Whether these discussions must be natural or uniform procedures have to be framed.

The Planning Board felt that all the voters would not participate in the Gram Sabhas, but persons ranging from 300-500 would be participating. There was a doubt whether these Gram Sabhas could be conducted effectively.

The Planning Board found practical solution to this problem. In spite of conducting Gram Sabhas as a big meeting it was decided to split it into small groups consisting of 50-60 members. These small groups would discuss among themselves and would report in the general meeting. In almost all the villages there is a school and if a school is selected as the venue of meeting and group discussion, it would be very convenient for all the people. The perceived advantage of this approach was that common people who might not be eloquent speakers especially ladies could actively take part in the discussions without hesitation.

Another suggestion which came up for the effective and efficient functioning of Gram Sabhas was to convene a meeting of the neighbourhood forums preceding to the convening of Gram Sabhas. Since these neighbourhood forums are more democratic and are having practical viability than Gram Sabhas, it could be used as forum for the articulation of local needs and demands.

The Functions of Special Gram Sabhas

The functions of the Gram Sabhas are classified into three:

1. To determine the various developmental problems in the village through discussion.

2. To ascertain resources and other details of the village through ward level discussions.

3. To render solutions to all the problems and to suggest measures for the optimum utilisation of new resources.

The discussions were to be conducted in small groups under twelve headings such as:

1. Agriculture and Irrigation
2. Animal Husbandry and Fisheries
3. Education
4. Drinking Water and Public Health
5. Industry
6. Transportation and Energy
7. Housing and Social Welfare
8. Culture
9. Women
10. Co-operative Sector
11. Welfare of the Scheduled Caste and Scheduled Tribe
12. Resource Mobilisation

How to Conduct the Discussions in Gram Sabhas?

The style of semi-structured questionnaire in rapid appraisal technique was followed in the discussions of Gram Sabhas. Two dozens of questions regarding the important problems and their solutions pertaining to that village were prepared and given. There was freedom to modify the questionnaire according to the conditions of the particular village. This questionnaire was not supposed to be given in the meeting but it had to be used as a helping tool for the person who leads the discussions. The questionnaire encompasses the various problems of the village. The person who leads the discussions has the duty to enable the people to examine the various problems in the light of their experience. One part of the questionnaire was to collect some information about related aspects in the village. These informations which can be collected only through survey or detailed assessments which is very tedious can be gathered easily through general discussions. These are the merits claimed in the initial stages.

The main objective of convening the second round of the Gram Sabhas was to prepare a plan document in accordance with the available resources and constraints of the particular local area, on the basis of the discussions conducted in the special Gram Sabha. The prime motive of convening the third round of Gram Sabhas was to accept the plan document and identify the beneficiaries based on the criteria decided by the Gram Sabha. The practical aspects of Gram Sabha would be discussed in detail later. The people's participation in the Gram Sabhas of Kerala are critically examined and analysed elsewhere.

From the above, it is clear that the State Government, the Planning Board and KSSP did everything possible to ensure maximum participation of the people in the Gram Sabha meetings as also to make the meeting most effective. What was the net outcome of all these efforts? Did people come out massively to attend Gram Sabha? What was the quality of the deliberations that took place in the Gram Sabhas?

To ascertain this the Planning Board data on Gram Sabha participation have been analysed. The participation of the people in the Gram Sabhas of two Blocks, *viz*., Vellanadu and Nedumangadu and one Municipality, *viz*., Nedumangadu have been examined to understand the nature and quality of participation.

From the tables below it can be seen that there is clear difference in the participation among districts in general as well as among the Panchayats in the districts. Districts of Thiruvananthapuram, Alappuzha, Idukki, Ernakulam, Malappuram, Calicut and Waynadu recorded above the state average of 179.67. The districts of Thiruvananthapuram, Quilon, Alappuzha, Kannur and Kozhikode are considered as left strongholds. Thrissure is predominantly left. In Ernakulam and Waynadu the strength of the left and non left forces are more or less equal. Kottayam, Idukki, Pathanamthitta and Malappuram are the bastions of non-left forces. In addition to Malappuram, Kasargod is also a strong hold of Muslim League. While looking at the data on participation one cannot find much differences in the level of participation between the left and non-left districts. Only in certain left controlled Panchayats, a slight edge over the UDF Panchayat is recorded.

Secondly, there were clear difference in participation in the Gram Sabhas among the Panchayats in all the districts. The Gram Sabhas of Pathiyoor Panchayat in the Alleppey district recorded a maximum participation of more than 1000 members. But the ironical fact is that the Gram Sabhas which recorded the lowest participation also belongs to a Panchayat of Alleppey district. These differences can be explained on the basis of the interest of the Panchayat committee to conduct Gram Sabhas and their organizing capacity. The participation in the Gram Sabhas was comparatively high in all those places where there was orderly work and organisation.

Table 4.1 : Districtwise Average Participation in Gram Sabhas in Kerala

District	Average Participation in Gram Sabhas	Women	SC/ST	Employees
Thiruvananthapuram	183.17	34.91	3.45	3.43
Kollam	178.21	25.14	4.13	8.90
Pathanamthitta	156.57	29.88	3.85	2.42
Alapuzha	205.26	29.35	3.45	7.38
Kottayam	148.36	23.85	2.60	7.38
Idukki	205.21	19.26	2.37	14.34
Ernakulam	189.79	19.04	1.94	8.34
Thrisuure	150.60	26.95	3 .17	0.61
Palghat	168.11	20.09	3.38	9.75
Malappuram	193.40	26.69	2.32	6.62
Calicut	214.18	27.72	0.41	0.00
Vaynad	215.58	19.99	2.40	8.73
Kannore	166.57	21.24	4.58	4.00
Kasargod	148.41	20.96	0.87	2.36
State Average	179.67	24.82	2.75	5.47

Source: Kerala State Planning Board.

The third inference from Table 4.2 is about the weakness of Gram Sabha. The main weakness of the Gram Sabhas was that there was no satisfactory participation from the part of Scheduled Castes and Scheduled Tribes. 25 per cent of the people who participated in the Gram Sabhas were women.

Table 4.2 : Average Percent of Voters Attending Gram Sabha 1 by Average Number of voters per ward

Size Class	Voters Per Ward		Population Density Per sq.km.	
	Number of Panchayats	Participation Rate	Number of Panchayats	Participation Rate
Less than 1,000	50	15.04	490	11.98
1,001 to 1,500	537	12.16	250	11.37
1,501 to 2,000	354	10.00	126	11.08
2,001 to 2,500	32	8.42	58	9.53
More than 2,500	6	7.55	53	8.61
Total	979	38	977	38

Source : Ibid.

The women's participation was comparatively high in all those places where the women were encouraged and given due consideration. In some Gram Sabhas the female participation was more than that of the males. The women were not mere spectators but actively took part in discussions. The subject group "women" was the most hotly debated theme. The highly controversial and contentious issues such as gender equality and cry for reservations were discussed and women expressed their feelings and emotions in this regard.

Table 4.3 shows that the Aryanadu Panchayat recorded the maximum participation and the Vellanadu Panchayat recorded the minimum participation. The main reason for this trend in participation within a Block can be attributed to the extent of urbanisation. Aryanadu and Poovachal Panchayats which recorded high participation retains the village character, whereas the Vellanadu Panchayat which recorded the minimum participation is having a high urbanizing trend. The other reasons for the varying trends in participation can be the interest and organising capacity of the Panchayat samitis. The participation of the employed cannot be termed as satisfactory. The major proportion of the participants who attended the Gram Sabhas belonged to the lower class followed by middle class. The participation of the upper class was negligible

Table 4.3 : Panchayatwise average participation of people in special Gram Sabhas in Vellanadu Block

Name of the Block: Vellanadu

No. of the Villages : 8

Name of the Village	Number of Wards Partici-pation	Average Female Partici-pation	Average Male Partici-pation	Average Total Partici-pation	Average Employee
Aryanad	11	116.09	175.45	291.54	3.45
Kattakada	13	67.76	105.46	167.23	10.15
Vidhura	11	67.91	117.82	185.73	3.82
Vellanad	11	48.18	86.36	134.54	2.09
Uzhamalackel	10	96.00	58.00	154.00	6.00
Tholicode	10	121.00	128.60	249.80	7.50
Poovachal	4	102.07	188.42	290.50	5.21
Kuttichal	9	72.33	76.55	148.88	0.77
Block Average	89	85.69	120.46	202.78	4.87

Source: Ibid.

Socio-economic and occupational status is an important reason behind the people's participation in Gram Sabhas. This phenomenon can be explained by considering the fact that the bulk of the participants of Gram Sabhas were people who were having burning problems and they considered the Gram Sabhas as forums for solving their problems. Can we attribute the low participation of the top strata of the society to their underestimation about the Gram Sabhas?

In the case of male participation, Poovachal Panchayat recorded the maximum and Uzhamalackal Panchayat recorded the minimum. Tholicode Panchayat and Vellanadu Panchayat recorded the highest and lowest female participation respectively. In all the Panchayats of Vellanadu Block, males exhibited more participation than females. This underscores the need for rendering attention for enhancing women participation.

Table 4.4 compares the participation of people in special Gram Sabhas and the II Gram Sabhas in the same Block. It is interesting to note that the participation of the people in the II Gram Sabhas were higher than the participation in special Gram Sabhas throughout the Block.

The participation of the employees has also increased slightly. The participation of the depressed classes has not come up to the

Table 4.4 : Panchayat-wise Average Participation of People in Special and second Gram Sabhas in Nedumangadu Block
Name of Block : Nedumangadu; Number of villages : 5

Name of	No. of	Participation in special Gram Sabhas					Participation in II Gram Sabha					
Panchayats	Wards	AMP	AFP	ATP	AEP	AMP	AFP	ATP	ASCP	ASTP	AEP	APBG
Anad	11	129.63	103.27	232.91	Nil	204.64	245.00	449.64	47.18	0.91	11.82	164.09
Aruvikkara	12	123.25	37.17	160.42	Nil	112.17	128.83	241.00	49.33	Nil	6.83	NA
Karakulam	14	127.14	33.86	161.00	3.79	212.43	176.64	389.07	43.70	Nil	5.86	90.07
Panavur	9	110.44	66.55	177.00	Nil	134.5	137.11	271.66	35.55	11.00	11.22	109.11
Vembayam	13	199.61	156.92	356.53	0.153	192.92	217.77	410.69	37.92	9.92	4.92	253.00
Block Average	59	138.01	79.55	217.57	1.97	171.3	181.07	352.42	42.75	7.57	8.13	154.08

Table 4.5 : Nature of participation in Gram Sabha

District	Average participation of voters			Average participation of Women			Average Participation of SC/ST		
	Gram Sabha I	Gram Sabha II	Gram Sabha III	Gram Sabha I	Gram Sabha II	Gram Sabha III	Gram Sabha I	Gram Sabha II	Gram sabha III
Trivandrum	11.24	9.68	15.75	34.86	41.30	54.28	17.39	19.61	20.37
Kollam	9.37	7.79	10.34	28.11	34.79	45.35	13.13	16.92	17.33
Pathanamthitta	12.62	8.92	14.13	29.12	33.34	43.05	13.29	24.70	23.72
Alappuzha	14.12	12.93	12.93	31.49	39.77	40.90	4.12	15.48	17.39
Kottayam	9.87	8.81	11.90	27.08	34.85	43.77	12.02	14.63	16.74
Idukki	12.51	10.39	11.29	22.45	23.26	29.46	16.87	21.17	26.08
Ernakulam	8.37	8.80	10.12	20.09	27.59	34.00	14.58	15.14	15.42
Thrissur	9.44	8.09	11.65	27.54	33.49	41.20	1.48	20.60	18.44
Palakkad	10.44	10.32	13.04	22.29	28.68	37.00	4.58	23.43	25.85
Malappuram	12.72	10.35	12.78	27.43	28.99	32.14	11.63	14.68	13.90
Kozhikode	15.32	13.59	11.08	26.76	28.60	36.78	—	11.95	12.24
Wayanad	13.98	10.82	11.45	22.39	25.75	33.73	16.15	17.01	—
Kannur	11.20	8.65	7.60	21.94	22.58	33.60	5.57	6.98	7.72
Kasargod	11.81	8.01	10.39	20.80	18.06	28.33	13.11	13.82	16.32
Total	11.40	10.10	11.86	26.19	30.27	38.29	8.82	18.26	17.45

expectations. The number of the people who participated in both the Gram Sabhas is very encouraging. The increased participation in the II Gram Sabhas can be attributed to the attitudinal change of the middle and upper class.

From Table 4.5, it can be inferred that the majority of the wards recorded more female participation than male participation. This is due to the special attempts made to ensure more female participation. Generally viewed, the figures of total participation is not upto the mark and this can be explained by underlining the fact that higher the urbanization, lower the participation. The SC/ST participation is also very low which calls for immediate action.

Table 4.6 : Wardwise Average Participation of People in the Second Ward Sabhas in Nedumangadu municipality

Name of Municipality: Nedumangadu; No. of Wards : 28

Ward Number	Average Male participation	Average Female participation	Average Total participation	Average SC/ST participation
1	190	156	346	44
2	171	135	306	92
3	48	83	131	1
4	113	68	181	57
5	51	115	166	53
6	80	34	114	1
7	85	120	205	31
8	120	73	193	27
9	—	—	—	—
10	92	137	229	56
11	60	87	147	24
12	64	1	65	0
13	56	35	91	33
14	94	15	109	16
15	103	159	262	31
16	88	120	208	138
17	49	62	111	12
18	60	80	140	51
19	96	117	213	36
20	119	149	268	57
21	65	83	148	25
22	76	68	144	3
23	102	103	205	46
24	113	72	185	51
25	32	57	89	51
26	86	92	177	37
27	106	111	217	15
28	112	102	214	31
Municipality Average	87.81	90.15	180.15	37.74

In the Nedumangadu Municipality almost all the other wards recorded a medium participation. This can be attributed to three reasons such as:

1. The nature of organising and interest taken in convening Ward Sabhas, in short the activism of local leadership;

2. The interest and awareness of the people about Ward Sabhas: and

3. Tthe geographic peculiarities of the ward and the employment pattern.

Table 4.7 compares the participation of people in special Gram Sabhas in Vellanadu and Nedumangadu Block Panchayats respectively. The female participation and employees participation are more in Vellanadu Block than in Nedumangadu. This can be attributed to the special interest taken by the Panchayat committees and the attitude of the people. The Nedumangadu Block recorded more male as well as total participation compared to the Vellanadu Block. The differences between the participation in two Blocks are not so big, by which it can be understood that same factors are responsible for the slightly varying trends in participation in both the Blocks.

Table 4.7 : Comparison of the average participation of the people in special Gram Sabhas in Vellanadu and Nedumangadu blocks

Name of Block	Average Male Participation	Average Female Participation	Average Total Participation	Average SC/ST Participation
Vellanadu	120.46	85.69	202.33	4.87
Neduman-gadu	138.01	79.55	215.57	1.97

Source: Kerala State Planning Board.

Table 4.8 gives a comparison between the Nedumangadu Block and the Municipality regarding the people's participation in second Gram Sabhas/Ward Sabhas. The main inference from the above table is that the people's participation in all respects in the Nedumangadu Block is higher than the people's participation in Municipality.

Table 4.8 : Comparison of the average participation of the people in Second Gram Sabhas in Nedumangadu Block and Municipality

Name of Block	Average Male Participation	Average Female Participation	Average Total Participation	Average SC/ST Participation
Nedumangadu Block	171.34	181.07	352.42	50.32
Nedumangadu Municipality	87.81	90.15	180.15	37.74

Source: Kerala State Planning Board.

The data clearly reveal that 11.38 per cent of the total electorate attended the special Gram Sabha meetings in connection with people's plan all over the state. The female participation rate is 26.22 per cent. SC/ST attendance is reported as 8.94 per cent. Data on second and third Gram Sabha meetings are also examined. There is no considerable increase in the rate of participation in the second and third Gram Sabhas. From an all India perspective 11.38 is an impressive figure. In majority of the States even after 10 years of the coming into existence of the new LSGIs the Gram Sabhas are not actually functioning. In certain States where it is functioning the attendance is very thin. However when we take into account Kerala's high level of literacy and high level of political participation, 11.38 per cent of attendance in Gram Sabhas are far from satisfactory. What could be the reasons?

The people's plan activists themselves have admitted the following in the matter of participation of people in the Gram Sabhas:

1. There is no increase in the rate of participation. The participation rate is more or less same in all the Gram Sabhas for which data are available;

2. Middle class and upper class did not attend Gram Sabha meetings;

3. The deliberations in Gram Sabha are of poor quality; and

4. Participation rate was high in the Gram Sabhas in which beneficiaries were identified.

This shows that the people of Kerala did not take Gram Sabha seriously. Why is it that the highly literate, highly politicized people of Kerala did not view the Gram Sabha positively and participate in it in a big way? The government and the Planning Board had resorted to all available methods to create awareness about the importance of Gram Sabha all over Kerala. Each and every individual in every nook and corner of Kerala came to know about Gram Sabha because of the massive campaign spearheaded by the Government, the Planning Board, the CPI(M) and the KSSP. Even then people of Kerala developed a cold feet towards the Gram Sabha.

Thomas Isaac made an attempt to identify the factors that he thought would have influenced the rate of participation. He considered demographic factors, historical-geographical factors, political factors and economic factors. He writes: "It must be noted that the results of the regression have low R-square values. This indicates that there are other important determinants of participation rates that are not captured in our data" (Isaac 2000:73). What are these other important determinants of participation?

Table 4.9 : Distribution of Gram Panchayats by Political affiliation of the Presidents and the Participation rate by District

District	Attendance at Gram Sabha 1 by District Political Front						
	No. of UDF Panchayats	% of Voters attending	No. of LDF Panchyats	% of Voters attending	No.of Other Panchayats	% of Voters attending	Total
Trivandrum	19	10.62	63	11.49	2	9.50	84
Kollam	13	10.49	58	9.13	0	0	71
Pathanamthitta	30	11.76	20	12.92	4	14.74	54
Alappuzha	31	13.69	40	14.45	0	0	71
Kottayam	40	9.50	24	9.92	9	11.70	73
Idukki	25	11.68	19	13.39	7	13.12	51
Ernakulam	39	8.27	45	8.41	2	9.86	86
Thrissure	40	8.53	58	10.95	0	0	98
Palakkad	26	9.37	61	10.96	3	9.14	90
Malappuram	55	11.85	28	14.64	11	11.21	94
Kozhikode	23	13.48	52	16.15	1	14.76	76
Wayanad	10	15.09	10	13.15	4	13.26	24
Kannur	25	10.15	54	11.15	2	10.10	81
Kasargod	15	12.03	15	12.86	7	9.12	37
Total	391	10.85	547	11.74	52	11.48	990

Notes : "Other" include 4 BJP-led Panchayats and 48 governed by various independents. Attendance figures are based on 972 panchayats.

Source: State Planning Board.

CPI(M) is the number one cadre party in the state and its mass strength has not eroded even in the context of set back to world communist movement in the aftermath of the demise of the Soviet Union. Its mass base is all encompassing. This is due to the kind of mass mobilisation that the party has been doing since 1964. EMS Namboodiripad said:

> Our greatest assets are our mass organisations and the democratic consciousness of our people. The combined strength of all mass organisations in the State is about ten million. Besides, there is a vast network of cooperative organisations and movements, such as the organisations of the library and literary movements. I am aware that there are some people who consider all these to be the bane of Kerala society. I have devoted my life to mobilising the people for radical transformation of our society, and I cannot but disagree with such perceptions. I feel that one big question that we face is whether the organised strength and political consciousness of our people can be used to increase production and productivity. I want to answer in the affirmative (EMS Namboodiripad 1994 as quoted in Thomas Isaac, 2000:26).

EMS is of the view that the strength of the mass organisations in the state can be used to increase production and productivity and in that way a new civic culture can be constructed. But actually what has happened in Kerala is the near total absence of the participation of mass organisations of the CPI(M) in any activity of the people's campaign. This is well documented by no less a person than EMS' son, E.M. Sreedharan, a Planning Board member during the left regime in Kerala. He observed that the mass organisations of the CPI(M) among farmers, agricultural workers, teachers, women, youth, etc. did not cooperate with people's plan. To further elaborate his argument he analysed certain cases. One of the major objectives of people's plan was to increase productivity in the agricultural sector. Gram Sabha provided an opportunity for both farmers and agricultural workers to work together and to deliberate deeply upon the problems in the sector and to suggest measures to overcome the crisis. However, in the words of Sreedharan, it was quite unfortunate that farmers organisations and agricultural workers organisations did not officially participate in Gram Sabha.

In the industrial sector, the emphasis of PCDP was on addressing the crisis in small industries and cottage industries. Even though Gram Sabha provided the platform to ponder over the problems in the sector, the attitude of trade unions was indifference and negligence. This is the case in other sectors including education, health, women development, etc. Why did mass organisations show indifference towards PCDP? They should have taken it seriously, because it was the duty of the mass organisations to address the development crisis and to participate in the activities to overcome it.

Moreover people in Gram Sabha should not be interpreted as a huddle. People are working in different sectors of production and distribution. Therefore all of them are members of one or other mass organisation. When they come to Gram Sabha as a member of a mass organisation, the vital link between Gram Sabha and mass organisation can be established. Unfortunately this kind of linking of Gram Sabha with mass organisation did not take place.

Sreedharan has tried to find out the reason behind the indifferent attitude of mass organisations towards Gram Sabha. Firstly, the mass organisations have developed a peculiar style of functioning since their inception. They have been working mainly on the basis of their understanding of the economic, social and cultural issues in the sector in which they have been working. For instance a union in the industrial sector would be organizing agitations to get their demands accepted. Similarly agricultural workers union, students unions, teachers organisations, women's associations etc. would be organising and articulating their demands through agitational methods. In other words the methods of all mass organisations are that of agitation. Secondly, the plan activists, instead of viewing people as people's power (through mass organisations) considered them as individual atom in the society. Due to this individual atom approach, PCDP activists did not make any attempt to mobilise mass organisations of the people (Sreedharan, 2000:247-61).

What Sreedharan said is true. If the mass organisation of CPI(M) actively participated in Gram Sabha, the participation rate would have gone beyond 50 per cent.

At this juncture any independent observer of Kerala politics and local democracy might be tempted to ask a question. Why CPI(M) did not mobilise its cadre to strengthen the Gram Sabha ? We cannot consider this as a lapse on the part of CPI(M). One of the underlying objectives of PCDP was to facilitate the further advancement of the left in the State (Thomas Isaac, 2000:35).

Thomas Isaac writes: Unlike left front in West Bengal, the Left Democratic Front in Kerala has not been in power continuously for a long period. Moreover, the strength of the CPI(M) within the left front has not been as decisive in terms of assembly seats. The CPI(M) has had only around half the LDF seats even though the CPI(M)'s share of voter support within the front is around 80 per cent. The formal vote share of CPI(M) in the total votes secured by the LDF has exhibited a clear trend of decline over time, even though by all indicators its mass strength has improved during the last decades and the mass support of some of the LDF partners severely declined" (*Ibid.*). He writes further: "By 1996, discussions and debates within the left [read CPI(M)] were bringing out ideas for a coherent strategy...... the centrepiece of the strategy was decentralisation with mass involvement to increase productivity in small scale sectors and to improve the quality of public services. The left (CPM) hoped this demographic response to the economic crisis would involve all political parties and sections of the people and help undermine the bipolar compartmentalisation of Kerala politics. The people so mobilized would be an extra-parliamentary pressure from below for efficient implementation of decentralisation. *The expectation was that the new strategy would facilitate further advance of the left in the state*" (*ibid.* : 35). From this it is clear that the CPI(M) wanted to mobilize those people at the grassroots level who are now not with CPI(M) or neutral to party politics.

The opposition Congress(I) understood the strategy of CPI(M) very well. It is evident from the statements issued by Congress leaders at the time of the commencement of the PCDP. The Congress party is also equally influential in Kerala society. In other words the political society of Kerala is sharply divided into two sections. The communist, anti-communist polarisation started in Kerala with the liberation movement unleashed by the non-left forces in the immediate aftermath of the first communist government assuming power in the state in 1957. This polarisation is a result of intense mobilisation by the leftists and the counter mobilisation by the non-left forces. The kind of mobilisation that we have noted here has politicised the entire society of Kerala. The CPI(M) is the number one cadre party in the state and it enjoys a hegemonic position in the society of Kerala through the party structure and the mass organisations. The CPI(M) has mobilised people in all walks of life and formed its own front organisations among students, teachers, government employees, workers, farmers, agricultural workers, traders, women, youth etc. The Congress party and its allies put together enjoy more or less equal support in Kerala society. The Congress is the rallying point for all the non-left social and political forces in Kerala. When the major parties and its front organisations are put together, their reach go beyond 80 per cent of the adult population of Kerala. We cannot find a society politicised and polarized to this extent in any other part of India. In Kerala no government programme, whether it is development scheme or welfare measure is non-political. Naturally the attitude of Congress and its allies towards a programme initiated by the CPI(M) government was lukewarm, if not negative.

However, the unimpressive attendance in Gram Sabhas has to be examined deeply. Before coming to that a cursory look at the nature and dynamics of Kerala's electoral behaviour would be useful. We have already noted that the political society of Kerala have engulfed more than 80 per cent of the societal space. We have also noted the neck-to-neck fight between the left and non-left political formations to establish their hegemony over Kerala society. But either the left or non-left have not been successful so far in establishing their supremacy. This is evident from the fact that political power in the State is alternated between the left and the non-left political formations in each general election. In the matter of elections to Union parliament the choice of Kerala electorate is the Congress front. When it comes to local body elections the left front comes out victorious in majority of the local self-government institutions. Thus the power balance in the highly politicized society of Kerala is tilted and a new equilibrium is created after every general election. The high level of mobilisation by the left forces mainly and the consolidation of the non-left forces behind the Congress have constructed a political society in which people are highly politicised and their participation in political activities are very high. At the same time, there exists a small arena of the non-political forces and that constitute the civil society of Kerala. It is the psyche of this civil society that is instrumental in the act of alternating of power between the left and non-left political formations in Kerala.

It seems that the civil society of Kerala did not favourably view the kind of local level democracy and local level development promoted by CPI(M). Kerala's civil society does not want to go the West Bengal way, where CPI(M) is the ruling party for more than twenty-five years. The CPI(M) achieved this in West Bengal through its grip over the rural areas in that state. The Kerala CPI(M) thought of a similar strategy to further enhance its influence in the state. They wanted to establish their ultimate control over the rural areas in Kerala through the participatory development programme. The civil society of Kerala which includes the psyche of the non-political sections of Kerala society is against all kinds of hegemonic designs, whether on the part of the left or the non-left. From the above we can safely say that the major reason that the Gram Sabha meetings could not attract people in a massive way is due to the apathy of the civil society of Kerala. In this context it is also to be kept in mind that the plan activists did not take into confidence the civil society organisations including NGOs, who are very actively involved in participatory development activities in several pockets of Kerala.

The above argument is substantiated by the elections to the local bodies in the fourth year of implementation of people's plan. (See Tables 4.10 and 4.11) CPI(M) lost majority of the urban bodies. It lost control over sizable number of rural local bodies also. In comparison to the 1995 position LDF lost 120 Gram Panchayats, 25 Block Panchayats and eight Municipalities besides one District Panchayat (Prabhash, 2000:204). In the next elections to the state legislative Assembly, the CPI(M) front was voted out of power. It is an irony that in the fifth year of the "decentralised planning with people's participation", the party that initiated the programme was thrown out of power democratically.

Table 4.10 : Number of Local Bodies Won by Fronts/Parties (1995-2000).

Local Bodies	Fronts / Parties								
	LDF		UDF		BJP		Hung		Total
	1995	2000	1995	2000	1995	2000	1995	2000	
Gram	556	436	344	374	3	3	87	114	927
Panchayats	(56)	(47)	(35)	(40)	(.3)	(.3)	(9)	(12)	(990)
Block	93	68	46	63	Nil	Nil	13	14	145
Panchayats	(61)	(47)	(36)	(43)			(7)	(10)	(152)
District	10	9	2	4	Nil	Nil	1	Nil	13
Panchayats	(71)	(69)	(21)	(31)			(7)		(14)
Municipalities	27	19	17	23	Nil	Nil	10	10	52
	(50)	(37)	(44)			(19)	(19)	(54)	
Corporations	2	2	Nil	1	Nil	Nil	1	2	5
	(67)	(40)		(20)			(33)	(40)	(3)

Notes : Figures given in brackets in the last column indicate that of 1995 election. *All other figures in brackets indicate percentage distribution.*

Source: J. Prabhash, *ISDA Journal,* Vol.10, No. 3, July-Sept. 2000, p. 203.

Table 4.11 : Percentage Distribution of seats by fronts (State total)

Front	Gram Panchayats	Munici-palities	Corpora-tions	Block Panchayats	District Panchayats
LDF	46.69	44.83	51.68	47.84	57.40
UDF	43.89	45.09	38.59	49.01	38.57
Others	9.42	10.08	9.73	3.15	4.04

Source: J. Prabhash 2000:204.

In the preceding paragraphs we have been trying to understand the nature and dynamics of Gram Sabhas in Kerala. The analysis presented here clearly shows that the people's participation rates in Gram Sabhas did not correspond to Kerala's high literacy rates and higher level of political participation. This is due to the non-involvement of mass organisations affiliated to CPI(M) as also the apathy of the civil society of Kerala.

In conclusion it can be stated that in the political society of Kerala the arena of the civil society is too small to be noticed. However this does not mean that the civil society is weak and meek. On the contrary it is vibrant and vigilant.

5

SUMMARY AND CONCLUSION

The present study is a critical evaluation of the mass movement launched by the LDF Government of Kerala to ensure people's participation in development process through the local self-government set-up. The study analyzed the constraints and possibilities in participatory planning and democratic decentralisation with special reference to Kerala. The study also tried to assess the role of civil society organizations in development process in Kerala.

To ensure popular participation in development planning, volunteers specially trained for this purpose sensitized people at the grassroots level. It is found that on an average 11 per cent of the total electorates participated in the special Gram Sabhas/ward conventions that were convened to articulate people's demands in sectors such as agriculture, health, education, industry, environment, depressed class and women development, irrigation and drinking water. Local Self-Government Institutions had drawn up their own separate 9th Plan proposals with popular participation and submitted to the district planning committee. The district planning committee prepared the district plan in tune with the separate plans of local bodies. Separate district plan proposal prepared by the district planning committee was submitted to Planning Board where it became the 9th Plan proposal of the State of Kerala. This is in fact a unique experiment in development process in India and this would give a new dimension to democratic de-centralisation experiments. However, participatory planning is a complex affair. It is a political process, which involves exercise of power by people as decision-makers. Therefore suitable political environment is required to enable and ensure people's participation in development process. Thus the suitability of the existing socio-political organisation of Kerala as facilitators of such a process in the present environment was examined. Organisations with rigid structures and concentration of power at the top found more difficult to devolve power to the bottom as it might affect their existing structures. In this context the role of political organisations are very important because they are involved in development issues whether in power or in opposition. Therefore any study of participatory planning would be incomplete without a proper understanding of the potentialities of political organisations in the process. Role of bureaucracy is also very important in this context. Bureaucracy is always reluctant to devolve power because they control the bottom and share the top. Bureaucracy affected the process of participatory planning significantly as (1) they were presently responsible for making decisions (along with politicians) and implementing them; (2) they maintained close interaction both individually and collectively with the political organisations; and (3) as a salaried group they were economically more powerful and influential at the local level.

Participatory planning at the micro-level could be hindered by individual or organised effort of the privileged groups of people working in the service and industrial sectors, particularly when the process involves curtailing or removing the privileges and power traditionally enjoyed by them. As a result the decentralised development programme by and large failed at the implementation stage. This is required to be analyzed against the backdrop of the nature of civil society in Kerala.

The Left Democratic Front (LDF) Government in 1996 initiated People's Plan Campaign (PPC) in Kerala. It is "a social movement which unfolds the latest episode in the state's experiments with democracy". The initiative came up in the context of 73rd and 74th Amendments to the Constitution of India. PCDP was formally inaugurated on 17th August, 1996.

The specific objectives of the Campaign were:

1. Decentralisation and people's participation had to be the hallmark of Kerala's approach to planning and development.

2. To ensure that the LSGIs prepared and prioritized a shelf of integrated schemes, in a scientific manner, so that programmes for the 9th Plan could be selected from them on a priority basis, and evolve functionally relevant and purposive people's participation.

3. Through the campaign it was aimed to break the atmosphere of cynicism that exists among the people today and instill in them a new sense of optimism and direction so that the mobilization of resources for the 9th Plan went beyond the traditional confines.

4. Through the campaign the whole process of the 9th Five Year Plan would be an instrument of mass education in regard to issues in development.

5. To tap new monetary, material and labour sources untapped or inadequately tapped for the implementation of local level plans.

6. To empower the LSGIs in the better performance of their functions especially in the process of implementation of sustainable development plans of their own. This could be possible only if they were provided with adequate finances, clear and unambiguous rules and related accounts and bureaucratic efficiency.

7. The campaign also hoped to achieve a perceptible impact in the implementation of the development projects not only in the manner of utilisation of funds but also in the accomplishment of construction based activities, ensuring social justice, accountability and the maximum of transparency.

8. To provide at the maximum of voluntary labour and social contributions to developmental activities. Participation of large sections of people in planning and implementation would no doubt strengthen the base of democracy. The perception of the people now is that governance is something, which can be undertaken only by officials.

It can be changed through large-scale participation of the people. People were given a chance to study about their villages. The underlying values of the campaign were acceleration of democratic decentralisation and transparency in public life. For the purpose, local bodies were empowered to meet the challenges of development at the grassroots. It is a supportive base to the concept of grama swaraj.

The Peoples Campaign for Development Planning (PCDP) tried to involve all sections of people irrespective of their political affiliations, religion, caste or gender in the process of local development from planning to evaluation.

The important steps in the PCDP were: (i) need identification in the Gram Sabha with people's participation, (ii) study of the land and people (situation analysis) to understand the relevant village realities, (iii) strategy setting, (iv) formation of task forces and projectization in which areas of development like agriculture, irrigation, social welfare, education, SC/ST development, cooperation, women development, public health, etc. were studied in depth and analyzed and action projects were prepared based on the process, (v) preparation of Panchayat/Municipal plan documents in which sectoral preferences were made to earmark at least 40 per cent to 50 per cent for productive sectors, 30-40 per cent for social services sector and 10-30 per cent for infrastructure development, (vi) plan vetting by Block Level Expert Committee (BLEC) to give projects proper form to ensure proper costing and phasing, etc., (vii) plan finalisation and release of plan assistance, and (viii) implementation.

Some other aspects are also worth mentioning in this context.

1. New public works rules were made to check corruption at the implementation stage of projects.

2. *Social auditing*: The financial transactions were made public through various ways. The public was allowed to ask for the details of expenditure, quality and quantity of materials used, the recognised plan, design of the work, estimate, etc.

3. *Monitoring*: A committee of five members including people's representatives, experts, officials and voluntary workers was constituted to see that the work was performed as planned.

4. *Community participation*: People's plan campaign was implemented through the newly formed constitutional structures of LSGIs. This enabled the PCDP to have maximum people's participation in all phases of implementation from planning to evaluation. Gram Sabhas were the statutory forum for the people to participate actively in the decision-making process on matters regarding their life and work. Democracy evolving from the bottom

of the social fabric is being exercised and continuously improved through the structures of Neighbourhood groups. In the implementation of PCDP, the Panchayat Committee was assisted by a planning committee, which received in addition to the support of academic committee the assistance of Key Resource Persons (KRPs), District Level Resource Persons (DRPs) and Local Level Resource Persons (LRPs).

The deliberations in the Gram Sabha were coordinated by Task Forces formed by the people for 12 sectors, *viz.*, Agriculture Development, Irrigation and Soil Conservation, Health and Drinking Water, Education and Culture, Housing, Energy and Transportation, Animal Husbandry, Women welfare, SC/ST welfare and Small scale industry.

In the present study the attempt has been to have a close look at the People's Plan Process including the nature and dynamics of Gram Sabha with a view to draw general conclusions about PCDP in Kerala.

Any evaluation of PCDP should be based on two major criteria:

1. Whether the projects formulated by local bodies strictly adhered to the sectoral allocation as envisaged and prescribed by the Planning Board.

2. The quality and sustainability of the projects implemented in various sectors.

Plan Implementation—Kudappanakunnu

Kudappanakunnu Panchayat is ruled by the Congress(I). During the first three years of People's Plan, the president of the Panchayat was a woman who got elected from a general constituency. The faction fight within the Congress(I) and the lack of interest in PCDP really affected the implementation of PCDP in this Panchayat.

The Development Reports of the Panchayat brought into light serious problems in all development sectors. However, the projects that were undertaken for implementation did not really reflect the needs identified by the people in Gram Sabhas and documented in

Development Report. The Development Report clearly identified the number of unemployed youths in the Panchayats. It had also discussed the problem of total stagnation in agricultural sector. However, no imaginative projects were undertaken and implemented for agricultural development. The severity of unemployment problem can be solved only by starting new industrial ventures. Even though Kudappanakunnu is in the suburb of Thiruvananthapuram City Corporation no industrial project worth the name was taken up. As we have already noted the State Planning Board instructed the Panchayats that they should earmark at least 40 to 50 per cent of the plan fund to productive sectors, *i.e.*, in Agriculture, Animal Husbandry, Fisheries and Small Industries. But productive sectors received only scant attention in Kudappanakunnu. Spending on productive sectors recorded a declining trend from 1997-98 to 2000-01. Even during 1997-98 this sector received only below 30 per cent. In 2000-01 it is below 5 per cent. Moreover the projects implemented in productive sectors are of low quality based on huge subsidies.

Projects taken up in productive sector recorded downward trend, in the four years under study, while infrastructure sector increased year after year. When Planning Board instructed to restrict the spending in this sector to 10 to 30 per cent, Kudappanakunnu was much interested in spending more on infrastructure sector. In 1997-98 the spending on this sector was above 15 per cent. In 1998-99 and 1999-2000 it was above 30 per cent. In 2000-01 it went beyond 40 per cent. All these spending have been for construction of new roads and repair of existing ones. It is interesting to note that all these works have been carried out by beneficiary committees. But field visits and enquiries by the present researcher revealed that all these beneficiary committees were *benami* committees of Panchayat level public works contractors.

One should not be blamed if one identifies nexus between the Panchayat committee and the contractors. When Planning Board directed to spend 30 to 40 per cent in social sector (Health, education, water supply, sanitation), Kudappanakunnu went beyond the above prescription. Only in 1997-98 the spending was little below 30 per cent. In 1999-2000 nearly 60 per cent was spent on social sector. In social sector also the favourite activities of the Panchayat were construction works in health centres, in schools, etc. Another sizeable portion went for purchase. Both the construction activity and purchase activity provided enough scope for swindling of public funds.

Women Development and SC/ST Development were priority areas of PCDP. But, in Kudappanakunnu, virtually no projects were implemented in women development sector. Data show that Kudappanakunnu spent apart from SCP fund and general plan fund for the development of SCs. In this way sizeable portion of the funds were directed towards construction activities in SC colonies.

In short, it can safely be stated that Kudappanakunnu by and large failed in fulfilling the objectives of PCDP.

Plan Implementation – Karakulam

Karakulam is a CPI(M) bastion and the Panchayat President was very active in implementing PCDP. The young and energetic Panchayat President with the support of his party and with the help of Kerala Sastra Sahitya Parishat (KSSP) could lead Karakulam to the position of the best Panchayat in Thiruvananthapuram District. Karakulam emerged as the best Panchayat in the District because of the consistent hard work by the Panchayat committee under the committed leadership of its President. It is worth noting that Karakulam could come out with certain unique models that could be emulated by other Panchayats in the State. Before enlisting these unique models, we could just summarize the nature of plan implementation in Karakulam.

It should be noted at the outset itself that, Karakulam was very careful to limit spending on infrastructure below the SPB prescription. The highest percentage of spending for this sector was in 1997-98 and it was only 15.97 per cent. At the same time Karakulam also failed in drawing imaginative projects in productive sector. The highest percentage of spending for this sector was in 1998-99. There were certain attempts from the part of the Panchayat to revive paddy cultivation. As a result of the direct intervention of the Panchayat, paddy cultivation had been extended to 6.5 hectares.

However, this was achieved through heavily subsidising paddy cultivation. Once the subsidy is withdrawn, cultivators would again stop cultivating paddy. A notable intervention of the Panchayat, in agriculture sector, is a project called "My Village Green Village" with the involvement of 7000 families; massive vegetable cultivation was initiated by the Panchayat. As a result vegetable production increased and now more than 250 families in the Panchayat took it up as their livelihood and started commercial production of vegetables. The advantage of this project is that even after the withdrawal of subsidy, the project could sustain at least through 250 families.

In animal husbandry Panchayat promoted mini dairy units and poultry farms. However, the sustainability of these projects was very much doubtful.

In the industrial sector, performance of Karakulam is also far from satisfactory level. Panchayat by and large failed to go beyond just registering an industrial cooperative society.

Karakulam has come out with certain commendable achievements in social sectors, particularly in education, water supply and housing. It is to be noted that Karakulam concentrated more on social sector. More than 50 per cent of the plan out lay went for social sector in 1997-98, 1998-99 and 1999-2000. In 1999-2000 the spending on social sector was 69.55 per cent. Only in 2000-01 the Panchayat spent slightly less than 50 per cent in this sector.

In education sector, the Panchayat intervened from pre-primary to technical education. Improvement of basic amenities in schools and improving the standard of education received the attention of PCDP in this Panchayat. Training for preprimary teachers, re-orientation for teachers, special coaching for SSLC students, information technology centres, rural resource centre, centre for arts and culture, project for the development of sports and games and so on are the important projects undertaken by Karakulam under PCDP. Of these rural resource centre and information technology centre are commendable achievements of Karakulam worthy of emulation by other panchayats.

In the health sector, the Panchayat had completed three ambitious projects, *viz.*, latrine for all, housing for all and drinking water for all. Latrine project was a highly subsidized one. Housing scheme was a project of the state government. Karakulam can be proud of the three drinking water projects it had completed. These drinking water projects are models for people's participation at all levels. Panchayat implemented several projects for the development of SCs. Houses had been provided to all SC families in the Panchayat. Houses in the *Laksham veedu* colonies were separated and remodelled. Drinking water projects were implemented for the benefit of SC colonies. Landless SC families had been allotted 3 cents of land.

The funds earmarked for SC development had been spent mainly in social and infrastructure sectors. No scheme had been launched for employment generation for the benefit of SCs. Karakulam has taken earnest efforts to address women specific development issues. This is evident from the fact that majority of convenors of *Ayalkootams* were women. This is really empowering women at the grassroots. Moreover, the Panchayat had established self-help groups in all wards.

The organisation base for people's participation is Gram Sabha. Gram Sabhas have been convened for both planning and implementation of projects. It is estimated that almost 11 per cent of the people participated in various meetings of Gram Sabha. This shows that people's participation in PCDP is not bad. However, when we look at the efforts taken by the Planning Board, and other activists in the PCDP to ensure people's participation, 11 per cent is not a satisfactory number. When we look at the nature and composition of those who participated, one fact could be noted that the middle class and the upper class abstained from coming to Gram Sabha.

However, the projects implemented in both the Panchayats were not meant exclusively for the poor and the marginalised. All the residents of the panchayats have a stake at the bridges, culverts and roads constructed in the nooks and corners of these Panchayats. Even then residents in the locality concerned remained to be apathetic towards the developmental works that were going on in their immediate vicinity. The reasons for this warrants further probing. Viewed thus stake holder involvement in various stages of planning, implementing and monitoring of different projects in various sectors and different areas in the panchayats studied was far below from what was conceived and expected.

However, Karakulam is comparatively better than Kudappanakunnu in ensuring people's participation. The activists of PCDP in Karakulam could stimulate at least a minimum number of people through the *Ayalkootams*. In Karakulam *Ayalkootam* emerged as democratic institutions of people below the level of Gram Sabha. It is not a small achievement that Karakulam established 174 *Ayalkootams* throughout the length and breadth of the Panchayat. This is not the case with Kudappanakunnu where one could not find massive mobilization of people through *Ayalkootams* network. A few *Ayalkootams* that were formed did not function properly.

We have already seen that in Karakulam, *Ayalkootams* functioned as democratic structures for people's participation at the grassroots even below the constituency of Gram Sabha. In due course these structures might evolve as organisations of direct democracy. Therefore it warrants a more detailed treatment.

Ayalkootam (Neighbourhood Groups)

As an agent of people's planning and development, *Ayalkootam* is the lowest unit in Kerala's contemporary democracy. 25 to 50 families in each Panchayat ward constitute one *Ayalkootam*. All adult members or voters in the locality are members of this democratic device. *Ayalkootams* are involved in all the developmental programmes in the Panchayat. For the formulation and implementation of each programme in Panchayat the ward members seek *Ayalkootam's* opinion.

People's participation in Gram Sabha might be for receiving benefits only, but they participated in *Ayalkootam*—mainly to become a part of the developmental process oftheir own Panchayat. "Power to the People" concept becomes meaningful only through participation of villagers in the developmental programmes or activities. For each *Ayalkootam* there was a Convener elected on democratic principles (nominating one person who won majority in that area). Besides participating in developmental programmes,it acts as an agent of interaction between Gram Sabha and people. It brings Panchayat's decisions and orders to the people and people's opinions and recommendations or even criticism to Panchayat. Thus, it is an eye to the Panchayat's policies by villagers. The dates and venues of Gram Sabha and Panchayat meetings are circulated among the people through this organisation. *Ayalkootam* convener's main duty is to ensure majority in Gram Sabha through campaigning about each meeting, agenda and purpose. Under each Gram Sabha there was 10 to 15 *Ayalkootams*. Most of the conveners of *Ayalkootam* were women; one of the main reasons for this situation is that they were in a position to find out enough time than men. According to Karakulam Panchayat President, only this kind of participation of women at lowest level could help the process of empowerment, which had been attempted to achieve through reservation. It is now easy to collect any details about Panchayat with in two or three days with the help of the *Ayalkootams*. Big programmes like Census or other information gathering has become easier and cheaper.

Providing leadership for implementing all the development scheme with in the Panchayat was with the *Ayalkootam*. For each project it constituted an organisational *samiti.* This *samiti* looked after every process regarding that particular project. One of the locals was elected as convener for that project. There was a monitoring committee to advise this organizational *samiti.* On project and Panchayat basis, there was a monitoring committee. With the advice of these committees *Ayalkootam* members organised and implemented projects. Another important duty of this *Ayalkootam* is to find out beneficiaries of different projects which gave financial aid to the people.

Karakulam Panchayat members were positive regarding *Ayalkootam's* role in the development process. There were 174 *Ayalkootams* in this Panchayat. Among them conveners of eighty *Ayalkootams* were women. Voluntary participation of women ensured the capacity of the Panchayat to mobilise and create awareness among women. If the Panchayat initiated an awareness campaign for women, it would turn as a Panchayat meeting with higher participation of women. Here the objective of higher participation of women in politics was achieved. In this Panchayat female participation was greater than male participation. According to its President, *Ayalkootam* in this Panchayat was more active than any other Panchayat. The Panchayat organised an awareness programme for conveners of Gram Sabhas and *Ayalkootams* in October 1 and 2 every year. In the training programme it was emphasised that the *Ayalkoottam* conveners and other elites, in addition to concentrating on development process, they should attend to other problems in their locality. Awareness on health and hygiene among people was a must to prevent the spread of dreadful diseases. For that common programmes for all villagers must be adopted on a similar basis, especially programmes like control of mosquitoes, rat, etc. Thus *Ayalkootam* could solve every problem which has a direct or indirect bearing on development, through creating awareness—which would be considered as the main duty of the *Ayalkootams*. Also it proved its potentiality as a grievance redressal mechanism at the grassroots level. In Kerala most of the civil cases filed in courts were on boundary disputes. These disputes could be settled easily through discussions within the *Ayalkootam*. *Ayalkootam* could solve such problems without spending a huge amount as court fee, advocate's fee, or fee of any other kind.

The performance of *Ayalkootam* in Kudappanakunnu is weak when compared to Karakulam. With the help of all political parties a *Janakiyavedi* or Democratic Centre was functioning here. Any number of celebrities and elites were residents of Kudappanakunnu, but they were not active members of *Ayalkootams*.

Among the two Panchayats *Ayalkootam* in Karakulam Panchayat is active. Karakulam is successful in a limited way in ensuring people's cooperation in decentralised planning through the *Ayalkootam* net work. Party differences, lack of awareness and enmity contributed to less success to people's participation in Kudappanakunnu Panchayat.

Concluding Observations

People's campaign for Development Planning in Kerala is definitely a revolutionary decision and bold step in the history of planned development in India. This internationally noted programme has received not only laurels, but brickbats also from different quarters; and it is quite natural considering the complexities and dimensions of people's participation in development. The data analyzed in the present study did not permit this researcher to be totally supportive. He has identified any number of strengths and weaknesses for the programme which has completed four years and entered into the fifth year of implementation at the time when this study was undertaken. It is very important to note that the LDF Government which initiated the programme was voted out and the UDF led by Congress(I) assumed power in the fifth year of implementation of People's Plan.

The most important feature that could be observed about the People's Plan initiative is that it has deviated considerably from the existing theories of People's Participation in Development in many ways. The dominant paradigm in the theoretical stream is the one currently propagated by the World Bank, where the emphasis is on the non-governmental organizations as the locomotive of People's Participation in Development. In PCDP, NGOs did not find any place. Instead, the constitutionally established Local Self-Government Institutions prepared their plans with people's participation. To mobilise people at the local level as a support system to LSGIs, the Popular Science Movement in Kerala (KSSP) took the lead role assisted by individual volunteers drawn from among School, College, University teachers and service organisations of state government employees, all affiliated to CPI(M). Here, it should be kept in mind that the teachers and government employees who participated in PCDP were not officially representing their sectoral organisations officially instead they actively participated in PCDP activities as members of KSSP. As we have already noted elsewhere the sectoral organisation of CPI(M) did not cooperate with PCDP. This is a deviation from the existing approach to People's Participation in Development where NGOs are given a prominent role for ensuring people's involvement. Independent academics who have undertaken studies on the role of NGOs have found that many of the NGOs are not sincere in their work in grass roots intervention. For the critiques of NGO's role, the new approach initiated in Kerala is an innovative one to be welcomed. In this way Kerala's PCDP has brought in considerable inputs for reconstructing the existing theory of people's participation in development.

In plan conceptualising, formulating, implementing, monitoring and evaluating of the projects, PCDP activists claim full success in ensuring total or near total participation of Gram Sabha. Gram Sabhas have to be convened four times a year as per the provisions of the LSGIs Acts of Kerala. However, we have already noted that People's participation in Gram Sabha did not go beyond 11 per cent. Said all these one should not lose sight of the fact that the 11 per cent who attended and participated in the Gram Sabha and PCDP are from the hither to marginalised and excluded sections of population at the local level. Notwithstanding the different interpretations, opinion is unanimous about the ultimate objective of People's Participation in Development as the most useful mechanism to reach to the ones who were excluded from the fruits of earlier attempts at development. Viewed thus as is evident from the nature of participation in Gram Sabhas , LDF government's programme of people's plan in a limited way contributed to the empowerment of the deprived and the marginalised.

However, the weaker sections did not participate in all the Gram Sabha meetings consistently. The participation was greater in the Gram Sabha, which was convened for the identification of beneficiaries. It takes us to the reality that people's effective participation was not available in formulating, implementing, monitoring and evaluating of the projects. The quality of the deliberations in the Gram Sabha was severely affected due to the total absence of participation of the upper class, middle class and the professional class in Gram Sabha meetings.

Why this? Kerala is well known for its social development. The people are cent-per-cent literate. Participation level of people in public activities are very high. For instance, voter turnout in general elections in Kerala are well above 70 per cent. The other features of Kerala are also to be taken into account. In this context Kerala society is a highly politicised one. The major portion of the social space in Kerala has been occupied by the CPI(M) and its front organisations. The trade unions, teachers organisations, employees organisations, women organisations, farmers organisations, agriculture workers organisations, youth and students organisations promoted and patronised by the CPI(M) are well entrenched in the society of Kerala.

The opposition to CPI(M) predominantly by the Congress(I), is also a force to be reckoned with. The Congress(I), its allies and front organisations are also strong enough, if not equal, to challenge the hegemonic position attained by the leftists. The net result is the near total politicization of the society and emergence of a bipolar pattern of coalition to alter power between these two coalitions in each general elections. In such a highly politicized society why did the people not come out in large numbers to attend the Gram Sabha meetings? The State Planning Board with the support of the LDF government launched a massive campaign programme to ensure maximum participation of the people in the Gram Sabhas. Street procession, theatricals, advertisements in newspapers, stills in electronic media and even door to door campaign by trained volunteers of KSSP failed to attract a sizeable section of the rural electorate to the people's assembly at the local level. Why? Thomas Isaac the principal protagonist of the PCDP tried to answer this question by analysing historical, geographical, demographic and political factors. He concluded that these factors did not decisively determine the level of participation in Gram Sabhas. It is conclusively proved that these factors really did not influence participation level. Throughout Kerala the participation rate is plus or minus 11 per cent. Then he admitted that the Planning Board data could not capture other determining factors.

The argument put forward by the CPI(M) leader and Planning Board member E.M. Sreedharan warrants our attention. He frankly admitted the fact that the mass organisations of even CPI(M) did not cooperate with Gram Sabhas. If the mass organisations wanted they could easily have made Gram Sabhas great events. From this one can easily infer that a section within CPI(M) did not favour strengthening of democracy at the local level through the mechanism of PCDP. Not only the mass organisations of CPI(M), the Congress and its affiliates also did not like further strengthening of Gram Sabha through the mobilisation process initiated by the Marxists controlled left government. The non-left forces did not like the CPI(M) making further in-roads into the rural areas in Kerala. The Congress and the non-left forces have already noted the peculiar pattern that emerged in Kerala through the electoral process all along these years ever since the formation of the state. The electoral trend in Kerala favoured the LDF in LSGIs and UDF in Parliament elections. In the state assembly elections power is alternated between these two fronts in each general elections.

It is very much clear from this electoral behaviour that the left in Kerala enjoyed a kind of dominance over the rural local bodies. The campaign was a mass mobilisation by the CPI(M) to further enhance the already existing hegemonic position.

The major objective of Kerala's People's Plan was to overcome the crisis that clouded, of late, the Kerala model of development. Any evaluation of People's Plan would definitely come to the conclusion that the People's Plan totally failed to overcome the development crisis the state has been facing. At the same time one cannot shut his eyes towards the fact that the campaign succeeded in mobilizing and organizing the marginalized sections at the local level into neighbourhood communities. These neighbourhood forums have the potentialities to resist the onslaught of globalisation in a limited way.

The important aspect of Kerala's development experience has been the intervention of the state to effect distributive justice. The significant aspect of this state intervention is that it is the response of the state to the pressures and demands of common people articulated through mass movements.

When we come to People's Plan one cannot observe such a demand articulation from any one of the mass movements in Kerala. PCDP is a programme of the state government without such a pressure from the masses. This is another reason for the failure of the programme.

Instead of hurriedly implementing PCDP, a mass movement should have been launched by the CPI(M) to mobilise people to participate in development programmes. Instead of the PCDP the left government should have devolved economic and administrative powers to the local bodies in a step by step way.The devolution scheme that was decided on the basis of the Sen Committee was good and the government should have made all attempts at the proper implementation of it.

The leftists in general and CPI(M) in particular can take the claim for organising all sections of the people in Kerala. The organisations of government employees, teachers, students and labourers are very powerful in articulating their sectarian demands. These organisations controlled mainly by CPI(M) are not prepared to make even minor sacrifices for the growth and welfare of the state as a whole. This has created a situation where the political society in Kerala is an arena pressurizing the government for achieving their sectarian demands.

The CPI(M) instead of the PCDP should have initiated a programme for "de-schooling" the mass organisations to open their eyes towards the larger development issues of the state. The situation in Kerala now is that the state has been witnessing a minimum of one *Bandh/Hartal* every month organised by political parties or politically affiliated mass organisations. As the number one cadre party of the state with its reach to all nooks and crannies of the state and whose ideology has an overwhelming influence upon Kerala society and polity, the CPI(M) should creatively think about a new development politics where sectarian interests should not get an upper hand. The beginning should be a "de-schooling" programme initiated by CPI(M) for its cadres and mass organisations that can greatly contribute the emergence of a civic culture where consensus could be arrived at without partisan bickerings on development issues, the pet theme of EMS in the last few years of his life.

The managers of PCDP reversed the sequence of

decentralisation process.They were well aware that decentralisation required a number of changes in the administrative structure and control over resources. They were also aware that a successful decentralisation have to put in place sequentially and with a clear demarcation of functions among the various levels of government. Administrative support structures have to be created be effecting institutional changes, redeploying staff, generating an information base, training personnel and establishing horizontal linkages among various agencies and departments. Awareness creation is also important (Isaac, 2000). Thomas Isaac further states: "There is little doubt that the administrative capacity and the experience of newly elected members of LSGIs did not warrant such a large-scale devolution. Instead of waiting for the gradual administrative capacity building through reform, the government opted to take the plunge and devolve the funds".While looking back now Thomas Isaac himself would be thinking that such a plunge without capacity building of the LSGIs was disastrous. Instead of "plunging and devolving funds" the LDF Government should have developed appropriate strategies for capacity building of LSGIs.

From the present analysis it has become quite clear that the campaign failed to achieve its declared objectives. The development crisis the state has been facing is so complex that it cannot be solved through the mobilisation of people at the local level. The campaign failed to mobilise the support of other major political parties and social formations to construct a new development compact. The strategists of the People's Plan could not even muster the support of other partners of the Left Democratic Front. It is also not a secret that a section in the CPI(M) itself did not whole heartedly support the campaign. Why did such a massive programme fail to achieve its declared objectives despite the fact that it was launched by the government of the left of which CPI(M) is a major partner.

There could be several reasons. One of the major reasons could be the failure of the strategists of PCDP in the CPI(M) to take into confidence even other partners in the Left Democratic Front. The CPI and RSP, two other important partners in the coalition were not that happy with the PCDP. Also PCDP activists failed to ensure the support of Kerala's civil society. No one can dispute the fact that CPI(M) is a cadre based mass party and its support base very strong and intact. Even though Congress party is not a cadre party, its support base is also as strong as that of CPI(M). Even though EMS and other important leaders of CPI(M) issued statements that we should have to shed our political differences in the matter of development of the state, no leader from the CPI(M) initiated a dialogue with the leaders of the Congress party before or after launching the programme. In Kerala social formations and their organisations have a historic role in achieving social development as also distributive justice. When a totally new development programme was launched by the left government, they should not have neglected the formidable social formations.

The social space of Kerala is occupied by any number of mass organisations, social movements and the NGOs. The managers of PCDP did not open a dialogue with the organisation that are not affiliated to CPI(M). This is the case with social movements and NGOs also. The only social partner in the campaign was the KSSP, the CPI(M) controlled popular service movement. Viewed thus the PCDP was a programme of a section with in the CPI(M) and they did not take into confidence other political partners, trade unions, social formations, new social movements and other such civil society organisations.

In the civic elections that was held in the fourth year of PCDP, CPI(M) lost control of sizeable number of rural local bodies and majority of the urban bodies. In the elections to the State Legislative Assembly next year, the CPI(M) front was voted out of power and the Congress party controlled UDF received a massive mandate of unprecedented nature in the electoral history of Kerala. This is in a way Kerala people's evaluation of the People's Plan.

BIBLIOGRAPHY

Acharya, Poromesh (2002): 'Education, Panchayats and Decentralisation: Myth and Realities', *Economic and Political Weekly*, Vol.37, No.8, Feb. 23, pp. 788-96.

Adam, Hochschild (1998): "Globalisation and culture", *Economic and Political Weekly*, May 23, pp. 1235-38.

Arnold, J. (1990*): Community Forestry Ten years of Review*, FAO, Rome.

Bagchi, A.K (1999): "Globalisation, Liberalisation and Vulnerability: India and Third World", *Economic and Political Weekly*, November 6, pp. 3219-30.

Bamberger, M.C. (1986): *Readings in Community Participation,* Washington DC, Economic Development Institute of the World Bank.

Bandhopadhyaya, D. (1997): 'People's Participation in Planning: Kerala Experiment', *Economic and Political Weekly*, Sep. 27, pp. 2450-54.

Bijukumar, V.C. (2000): 'In Response to Development Crisis: Decentralised Planning and Development in Kerala', *Journal of Rural* and Buijs (Eds). *The Participation of the poor in Development*, Leiden Institute of Cultural and Social Studies.

Buijis, H. (1982): 'The Participation process: When it starts in Galjart Chambers R (1993): *Challenging the Professions*, IT Publications, London.

Burkeys (1993): *People First: A Guide to participation in Rural Development*, Zed publications, London.

Carroll (1992): *Intermediary NGOs*, Kumarian Press.

Carroll (1994): *Intermediary NGOs and Participation*, Manuscript, World Bank.

Cernea, M. (1989): *Non Governmental Organisations and Local Development*, Washington DC, World Bank.

Chambers, R. (1983): *Rural Development Putting the last first,* Longmans.

Chambers, R. (1989): *Farmer First: Farmer Innovation and Agricultural Research* UK, Intermediate Technology publications. *Development*, Vol. 19, No.3, July-Sep., pp. 353-69.

Chathukulam, Jos and Jose, T. Thomas (1997): 'Power to the People: People's campaign for the Ninth Plan in Kerala', *Kurukshetra*, Vol.45, No. 9, June, pp. 34-39.

Chathukulam, Jos and V.K. Kurian (1995): *Participation of Rural poor in Rural development and delivering systems: A case study of Jawahar Rozgar Yojana in Kerala*, Centre for Rural Management.

Chathukulam, Jos and M. S. John (1998): *Sen Committium Panchayat Rajum* (Malayalam) Centre for Rural Management, Kottayam, Kerala.

Choudhury, R.C. (2000): *Participatory Development: A Case for Civil Society and Panchayati Raj Collaboration*, State Planning Board, Kerala.

Clarke, J.C. (1991): *Democratising Development: The Role of Voluntary Organisations*, Earth Scan, London.

Clayton, A. (1994): *Governance, Democracy and Conditionality what role for NGO's*?, INTRAC, Oxford.

Cohen, J.M. and Uphoff, N. (1977): *Rural Development Participation*: University of Cornell.

Crouch, B. and Chamala, S. (1979): *Agricultural Extension and Education*, John Wiley, UK

—— (2000a): *Thakararu Janakeeyasuthranathinalla: Vikendrijaranathe Sambandhicha Kazhchappadinanu* (Mal), Centre for Rural Management, Kottayam.

—— (2000b): 'Empowertment of women panchayat members: Learningfrom Kerala (India); *Asian Journal of Women studies*, Vol.6, No.4, p.p 66-101.

Chattopadhyay, S. (2001): 'Resource Mapping for Decentralised Planning: Lessons from Kerala', Paper presented at the workshop on Decentralisation in Kerala. An assessment Oct. 22-24, KRPLLD, Centre for Development Studies, Thiruvananthapuram.

Cousins, Tessa (1998): 'Giving space to conflict in Training' in Irene Guit and Meera Kaul Shah (eds). *The Myth of Community: Gender Issues in Participatory Development*, Vistaar, New Delhi, pp. 58-70.

Crook, Richard C. and James, Manor (1998): *Democracy and Decentralisation in South Asia and West Africa: Participation, Accountability and Performance*, Cambridge University Press, Cambridge.

Das, M.K. (2000): 'Kerala's Decentralised Planning: Floundering Experiment', *Economic and Political Weekly*, Dec. 2, pp. 4300-03.

Das Gupta, P. (1990): "When being and the Extent of its realization in poor countries", *Economic Journal*, Vol.100, No.400, Cambridge.

Devika, J. and Praveena Kodoth (2001): 'Sexual Violence and Predicament of Feminist Politics in Kerala', *Economic and Political Weekly*, Vol. 36, No.33, Aug. 18, pp. 3170-77.

Devitt, P. (1980): *Poverty Focused Rural Development*, ODI, London.

Dichter, T.C. (1992): 'Demystitying Popular Participation' Bhatnagarand Williams (Eds). *Op.cit.*

Dreeze, J. and Sen, A.C. (1989): *Hunger and Public Action*, Clarendon Press, Oxford.

ECA (1990): *African Charter too popular participation*, ECA, Addis Ababa.

Elliot, C.C. (1976): *Patterns of poverty in the Third World*, Praeger, London.

ERDEA (1990): *Evaluation of Rural Development*, Rome, FAO.

Falk Richard (1995): *On Human Governance*, Polity Press.

FAO (1981): *The peasants Charter*, Rome.

FAO (1983): *Development strategies for the Rural Poor*, Rome.

FAO (1987): *The Impact of Development Strategies on the Rural Poor*, Rome.

FAO/SIDA (1987): *Restoring the Balance: Woman and Forestry Resources*, Rome.

FAO/SIDA (1989): *People's Participation in Agriculture and Rural Development*, Rome.

Farringdon, J. and Martin, A.C. (1987): *Farmer Participation in Agricultural Research: A Review of Concepts and Practices*, Overseas Development Institute, London.

Farringdon, J. and Bebbington, A. (1993): *Reluctant Partners: NGOs ,the State and sustainable agriculture*, Routledge, London.

Fernandez, W. and Tandon, R. (1986): *Participatory Research and Evaluation*, Indian Social Institute, New Delhi.

Feurstein, M.T. (1986): *Partners in Evaluation*, Macmillan, London.

Fowler, A. (1988): *Non-Governmental Organisation Achieving Comparative Advantage*, Institute of Development Studies, Sussex.

Fowler, A. (1990): 'Doing it better', *AERDD Bulletin*, No.28, University of Reading.

Franke, Richard W and Barbara H Chasin: 'Power to the Malayalee People', http:11chss.mantclair.edu/antro/Z97.html

Freidmann, J. C. (1992): *Empowerment: The Politics of Alternative Development*, Blackwell, Oxford.

Freire, P. (1972): *Cultural Action for Freedom*, Penguin, London.

Fukuyamam, Francis (1992): *The End of History and the Last Man*, New York, The Free Press.

Ghai, D.C. (1988): *Participatory Development: Some perspectives from Grass Roots Experiences,* UNRISD, Geneva.

Govt. of India (1963): *Report of the Study Team on the Position of the Gram Sabha in Panchayat Raj Movement*, Ministry of Community Development and Cooperation, New Delhi.

Govt. of Kerala (2002): *Economic Review 2001*, Kerala State Planning Board, Thiruvananthapuram.

—— (1997): *Report of the Committee on Decentralisation of Powers*, Government Press, Thiruvananthapuram.

GTZ(1987): *Rural Finance: Guiding Principles*, Eschhorn, Germany

Haaue, W. *et.al* (1979): 'Towards a theory of Rural Development', *Development Dialogue*, No.2, Uppsala.

Hatch, J. (1983): *A manual for participatory Evaluation in community based enterprises,* Technoserve Inc, New York.

Huntington, Samuel P. (1996): *The Clash of Civilisation and the Remaking of World Order*, New York: Simon and Schuster.

ILO (1981): *Structure and Functions of Rural workers organisations*; Geneva.

ILO (1987): Workers Education for the strengthening and Development of RWOs and their participation in Rural Development, Geneva.

ILO (1987): *Rural Development and Women: Lessons from the field*, Geneva.

ILO (1990): *The Socio-economic impact of Technical Cooperation projects concerning Rural Development*, Geneva.

Isaac, Thomas T.M. and L.N. Harilal (1997): 'Planning for empowerment: People's Campaign for decentralized planning in Kerala, *Economic and Political Weekly*, Vol.32, No.1, Jan 4, p.p53-58.

Isaac, Thomas T.M. with Richard Franke (2000): *Local Democracy and Development: People's campaign for decentralized Planning in Kerala*, Letword, New Delhi.

Isaac, Thomas T.M. (1997): *Janakeeyasuthranam: Sidhantavum Prayogavum* (Mal), State Planning Board, Thiruvananthapuram.

Isaac, Thomas T.M. and E.M. Sreedharan (2002): *E M Sum Adhikaravikendrikaranavum* (Mal), Chintha Publishers, Thiruvananthapuram.

Isaac, Thomas T.M *et al.* (1995): *The Kalliasseri Experiment*, KSSP, IRTC, Palakkad.

James, Petras (1999): "Globalisation: A socialist Perspective", *Economic and Political Weekly*, February 20 pp. 459-63.

Janardhan, V. (1997): "Globalisation of Capital, Multinational Corporation and Labour", *Economic and Political Weekly*, August 30, pp. L.2-L.9.

Jeffrey, Robin (1993): *Politics, women and well being, How Kerala became a model*, Delhi, Oxford.

John, M. Hobson (1997): *The Wealth of States*, Cambridge University Press.

John, M.S. (2000): 'Decentralised Planning and Employment Generation: Case Study of a village Panchayat in Kerala', *Kurukshetra*, Vol.48, No.7, (Special Issue), pp. 32-38.

John, M.S. and Chathukulkam Jose (1999a): "The Relationship between Gram Sabha and Gram Panchayat', *Kurukshetra*, Vol.48, No.1, Annual Issue, pp. 40-45.

——(1999b): 'Decentralised Planning and Panchayats in Kerala', *Kurukshtera*, Vol.47, No.12, Sep, pp. 20-23.

——(2001a): 'Decentralised Planning and Growth in the productive sectors: Case study of a village Panchayat in Kerala', Paper presented at the convention on Development, Nov. 16-18, Madras Institute of Development Studies, Chennai.

—— (2000b): 'Gender issues and participatory Planning: case presented at the workshop on decentralization in Kerala: An assessment Oct. 22-24, KRPLLD, Centre for Development studies, Thiruvananthapuram.

——(2002): 'Building social capital Through State Initiative: The case of participatory Planning in Kerala', *Economic and Political Weekly*, Vol37, No.20, May 18, pp. 1939-48.

Kannan, K.P. (2000): 'People's Planning: Kerala's Dilemma', *Seminar*, No.485, Jan.

Kenneth, Keniston (1998): "Political Culture and Software", *Economic and Political Weekly*, January 17, pp. 105-10.

Korten, F. and Siy R (1989): Transforming Bureaucracy: The Experience of the Philippine National Irrigation Administration: Bculder Westview, Press.

KSSP (2002): *Jankeyasuthranam, Anubhavangalum Adiyanthira Kadamakalum* (Mal), Cochin.

Kurian, Luciamma (2001): *The structure and Functioning of Gram Sabha: A study focused on the District of Kottayam*, Unpublished PhD Thesis, Mahatma Gandhi University.

Mahi, Pal (2001): 'Documenting Panchayat Raj', *Economic and Political Weekly*, Vol36, No.36, Sept 8-14, pp. 3448-50.

Manjula, B (2000): *Voice from the Spiral of Silence: A Case Study of Samatha Self Help Groups of Ulloor,* State Planning Board Kerala.

Manu, Shroff (1999): 'Globalisation: A Stock -- Taking', *Economic and Political Weekly*, October 2, pp. 2845-49.

Michael, Edwards (1999): *Future Positive*, Earth Scan Publications Ltd.

Midgeley, J.C. (1986): Community participation, *Social development and the state,* Methuen, London.

Mohanan, B. (1995): *Globalisation of Economy*, Gyan New Delhi

—— (1999): *Quest for a Just World Order*, ISDA, Trivandrum.

—— (1996): "Democratic Decentralisation in India: impediments and potentialities", *ISDA Journal*, VOl.6, No.1.

—— (2000): "From Economic Globalisation to Post Globalised Societal Order and the Indian State", *ISDA Journal* Vol.10, No.3, July-September.

—— (2003): "Decentralised Planning and Development", *South Asia Politics* Volume 2, No.3 pp. 36-42.

Mohankumar, S. (2002): 'From People's Plan to Plan Sans People', *Economic and Political Weekly*, Vol.37, No.16, April 20-26, pp. 1492-97.

Muraleedharan, K. (2000): *Dynamics of Women's Participation in Development : The Kerala Experience*, State Planning Board, Kerala.

Nagle, W. and Ghasa, S. (1990): *Community Participation in World Bank Supported Projects,* Washington DC.

Narain, Iqbal (1962): 'Gram Sabha and Panchayat Raj', *Political Science Review*, Vol.1, pp. 218-24.

Narayananas, M.G.S. (1997): 'The concept of Decentralisation: Expectations, Limitations and Possibilities', in NP Chakkutty (ed), *The Peoples Plan: A Debate in Kerala's People's Planning Experiment,* Calicut Press Club, Calicut, pp. 13-29.

Nossiter, T.J. (1982): *Communism in Kerala: A study in Political Adaptation*, Oxford University Press, New Delhi.

Nyoni, S. (1989): 'People's Power in Zimbabwe' in *Breaking the monopoly of knowledge*, ILO, Geneva.

Oakley, P. (1989): *Community Involvement in Health Development*, WHO, Geneva.

Oakley, P. (1991): *Projects with People: The practice of Participation*

OECD (1988): *Voluntary Aid for Development: The Role of Non Government Organisations*, Paris.

OECD (1994): *Promoting Participatory Development: From Advocacy to Action*, Paris.

Ogun, B. (1990): *Particpatory Development.*

Paul, T.V. and John A. Hall (1999): *International Order and the Future of World Politics*, Cambridge University Press.

Pearse, A. and Stiejel, M. (1979): *Inquiry into Participation*, Geneva.

Rajni, Kothari (1993): "The Yawning Vacuum: A World Without Alternatives", *Alternatives* 18(2), pp. 119-39.

Rehunandan, V.R. (2001): 'Micro level organisations: New Forms of Social Capital', Paper presented at the workshop on decentralization in Kerala: An Assessment, Oct. 22-24, KRPLLD, Centre for Development Studies, Thiruvananthapuram.

Reghuram, Sobha (2000): 'Kerala's Democratic Decentralisation: History in the Making, *Economic and Political Weekly*, Vol.35, No.25, June 17, pp. 2105-07.

Rahman, A. (1982): *The theory and practice of participatory Action Research*, ILO, Geneva.

Rahman, A. (1990): 'People's Development; *Community Development Journal*, Vol,25, No.4, Oxford.

Rahman, A. (1993): *People's Self Development*, Zed, London.

Richards, M. (1985): *The Evaluation of Cultural Action*, Mac millan, London.

Richards, P. (1985): *Indegenous Agricultural Revolution*, Hutchinson, London.

Samir, Amin (1997): *Capitalism in the age of Globalisation*, Madhyam Books, New Delhi.

Samir, Amin (1998): 'Towards a Progressive and Democratic New World Order', *Economic and Political Weekly*, June 6, pp. 1385-90.

Samir, Amin (2000): "The Political Economy of the Twentieth Century", *Monthly Review*, Vol.52, No.2, pp. 1-17.

Seema, T.N. and Vanitha Mukherjee (2000): *Gender, Governance and Citizenship in Decentralised Planning*, State Planning Board, Kerala.

Siriwardena, S. (1989): *From Planned Intervention to Negotiated Development*, Wageningen University, Netherlands. Smith K. International Child Development Centre, UNICEF.

United, Nations (1989): *National Experience in Promoting the cooperative movement*, New York.

UNDP (1990): *Human Development*, New York.

Uphoff, N. (1990): *Farmer Participation in Improving irrigation system management for sustainable agriculture in Asia*, FAO, Bangkok.

Van, Heck B. (1990): *Participatory Development: Guidelines for beneficiary participation*, FAO, Rome.

Van, Heck B. (1990): *Participation of Rural Poor in Development Through self-formed Groups and organisations*, FAO, Rome.

Wade, R. (1982): *Irrigation and Agricultural Politics in South Kerala*, Westview, Colorado.

Wade, R. (1987): 'The Management of common property Resources: Findings a cooperative solution', *Research observer*, Vol.2, No.2, World Bank.

World Bank (1988): *Rural Development: World Bank experience 1965-86*, Washington DC.

World Bank (1990): *Strengthening the Banks worlds on popular participation*: Washington DC.

World Bank (1994): *Report of the learning group on participatory Development*, Washington DC.

INDEX